The First-Year Experience
Monograph Series No. 42

Exploring the Evidence:
Reporting Research on First-Year Seminars
Volume III

Barbara F. Tobolowsky, Bradley E. Cox, and Mary T. Wagner
Editors

NATIONAL RESOURCE CENTER
THE FIRST-YEAR EXPERIENCE
& STUDENTS IN TRANSITION
UNIVERSITY OF SOUTH CAROLINA
2005

Cite as:

Tobolowsky, B. F., Cox, B. E., & Wagner, M. T. (Eds.). (2005). *Exploring the evidence: Reporting research on first-year seminars, Volume III* (Monograph No. 42). Columbia, SC: University of South Carolina, National Resource Center for The First-Year Experience and Students in Transition.

Sample chapter citation:

Friedman, D. (2005). Appalachian State University. In B. F. Tobolowsky, B. E. Cox, & M. T. Wagner (Eds.), *Exploring the evidence: Reporting research on first-year seminars, Volume III* (Monograph No. 42) (pp.13-17). Columbia, SC: University of South Carolina, National Resource Center for The First-Year Experience and Students in Transition.

Additional copies of this monograph may be ordered from the National Resource Center for The First-Year Experience and Students in Transition, University of South Carolina, 1728 College Street, Columbia, SC 29208. Telephone (803) 777-6229. Fax (803) 777-4699.

Special gratitude is expressed to Jenny Anderson, Composition Assistant, for design; Michelle Mouton, Editorial Assistant, for copyediting and layout; Inge Lewis, Editor, for proofing assistance; Tracy L. Skipper, Editorial Projects Coordinator, for copyediting; and Carrie Linder and Marla Mamrick for acquisition and selection of submissions.

ISBN: 1-889271-50-0

Exploring the evidence. Volume III, Reporting research on first-year seminars / Barbara F. Tobolowsky, Bradley E. Cox, and Mary T. Wagner, editors.
    p. cm. -- (The first-year experience monograph series ; no. 42)
  Includes bibliographical references and index.
  ISBN 1-889271-50-0
  1. Seminars. 2. College freshmen--United States. 3. Universities and colleges--Curricula--United States. I. Title: Reporting research on first-year seminars. II. Tobolowsky, Barbara F. III. Cox, Bradley E. IV. Wagner, Mary T. V. Series.
  LB2393.5.E96 2005
  378.1'98--dc22
                    2004027810

Contents

# Introduction

It has often been said that the first-year seminar is the most researched innovation in higher education. The seminar has been researched to encourage its development, validate its use, support its growth, and guide its improvement. This is the third volume of campus-based research on the first-year seminar that the National Resource Center for The First-Year Experience and Students in Transition has collected. The first compendium was published in 1993.

Since that first volume 11 years ago, the seminar has undergone many changes. One of the unique developments is the inclusion of the seminar in learning communities. Several of the institutions included in this volume assessed their seminars as part of this unique structure. However, not all aspects included here are new. Much of the research in this volume, as in the past, focuses on how the seminar increased retention to the second year and to graduation. Other issues addressed include grade point average, student satisfaction and engagement, and student achievement of course goals (e.g., use of advising and tutoring, awareness of social justice, increased interaction with peers and faculty).

As the nature of first-year seminars has changed since 1993, so too has the nature of assessment. Commercially available instruments to assess the first year of college, such as the First-Year Initiative benchmarking survey, the National Survey of Student Engagement (NSSE), and the Your First College Year (YFCY) survey, have become popular assessment tools. The changing assessment landscape is reflected in several of the submissions that report findings from these external instruments. However, most of the institutions report findings from their own campus-designed research tools.

We thank all institutions that submitted research for inclusion in this monograph. We recognize the effort that went into the initial research (not to mention writing up the findings for this monograph) as well as the risk in exposing these efforts to review and critique. The final result is 39 studies conducted on first-year seminars from around North America at two-year and four-year, and public and private institutions.

Further, we hope the monograph is user-friendly. To that end, the institutions are listed alphabetically. In addition, to help readers find programs similar to their own, each entry contains a note listing the type and control of the institution, institutional size, seminar type, and, if applicable, if the seminar is embedded in a learning community. We have also supplied several different indexes to assist readers in locating similar courses, institutions, and outcomes. Finally, we hope this resource continues the long-standing tradition of using research to establish, improve, and institutionalize the first-year seminar.

Barbara F. Tobolowsky
Bradley E. Cox
Mary T. Wagner

 # Key to Institutional Sidebars

Each institution's title page includes a sidebar that presents a snapshot of the institution and its seminars so that readers can locate institutions and courses comparable to their own. The data presented in the sidebar are more fully explained in the text of each accompanying article. To help readers understand the language used throughout the monograph, we have included a brief explanation below.

Information presented in the sidebar includes:

Example	Description
Abilene Christian University	Institution
Abilene, TX	Location
Private, Four-Year	Institution Control and Type
4,648	Institutional Size
Extended Orientation	Seminar Type (see explanation below)
Learning Community	Institutions in which some or all of the seminar sections are linked to other courses

Institutional Size

Enrollment information is for fall 2003 and is taken from the *2005 Higher Education Directory*. Enrollment information for the University of Calgary comes from the University's 2003-2004 Fact Book.

Seminar Types

As part of her dissertation research, Barefoot (1992) created a typology of five distinct seminar types. The 1991 National Survey of First-Year Seminar Programming (Barefoot & Fidler, 1992) relied on these definitions, and the seminars included in this monograph are described using similar terminology. Those types are:

1. *Extended orientation seminar.* Sometimes called a freshman orientation, college survival, college transition, or student success course. Content likely will include introduction to campus resources, time management, academic and career planning, learning strategies, and an introduction to student development issues.
2. *Academic seminar with generally uniform content across sections.* May be an interdisciplinary or theme-oriented course, sometimes part of a general education requirement. Primary focus is on academic theme/discipline but will often include academic skills components such as critical thinking and expository writing.

3. *Academic seminars with variable content.* Similar to previously mentioned academic seminar except that specific topics vary from section to section.
4. *Pre-professional or discipline-linked seminar.* Designed to prepare students for the demands of the major/discipline and the profession. Generally taught within professional schools or specific disciplines.
5. *Basic study skills seminar.* The focus is on basic academic skills such as grammar, note taking, and reading texts. Often offered for academically underprepared students.

Institutions that offer seminars combining elements of more than one seminar type are labeled as *hybrids.*

References

Barefoot, B. O. (1992). *Helping first-year college students climb the academic ladder: Report of a national survey of freshman seminar programming in American higher education.* Unpublished doctoral dissertation, College of William and Mary, Williamsburg, VA.

Barefoot, B. O., & Fidler, P. P. (1992). *1991 national survey of freshman seminar programming.* (Monograph No. 10). Columbia, SC: University of South Carolina, National Resource Center for The Freshman Year Experience.

Abilene Christian University

The Institution

Abilene Christian University (ACU) is a private, four-year institution in Abilene, Texas. Academic offerings include more than 70 baccalaureate majors, 26 master's programs, and one doctoral program. Affiliated with Churches of Christ, ACU stresses strong academics with Christian values.

Enrollment is approximately 4,700, 90% being full-time students with an average age of 22 years. The male/female proportion is 48% and 52%, respectively. The majority of students (80%) are White; 6.4% are African American, 6.0% Hispanic, and 3.8% non-resident students. All first-year students live on campus. Approximately 25% of the entering class are undecided majors, and 18% are first-generation college students.

The Seminar

ACU's first-year course, *University Seminar* (U100), is an extended orientation seminar that strives to build community; explore campus heritage and culture; provide career, academic, and personal advice; teach study skills; and confirm a major. Offered since 1989, it is designed to teach college success skills and to ease the transition to college life. It is a one-semester, one-credit-hour course required of all first-year and transfer students. Most sections are for students of any major, but a few discipline-specific, honors, or learning community sections are offered. Typically, ACU offers 56 U100 sections each year. With a maximum class size of 22, approximately 980 students take the course annually. University faculty or staff with master's degrees teach the course.

Sample course topics include the history of the university, integrating faith and learning, decision making, learning styles, critical thinking, and careers. All sections cover a standardized list of topics, but instructors can adapt or expand exercises within topics to meet the needs of their students.

Institution Profile:

Abilene, TX

Private, Four-Year

4,648

Extended Orientation

Learning Community

One of the required U100 components is library skills. Librarians, in partnership with course instructors, develop the library unit and instructional strategies. The goals of the library unit are to introduce beginning information literacy concepts and to teach students how to use the library catalog and a basic periodical index. The unit typically consists of three parts: (a) an introductory exercise to the library catalog that students complete on their own, (b) a class library visit designed to teach advanced searching skills, and (c) a follow-up research activity where students apply what they have learned. When covering the library skills unit, the classes meet in the library computer lab, and the librarian acts as guest instructor.

Research Design

This longitudinal study examines the effectiveness of several instructional methods for teaching library skills. Over an eight-year period, we tried three separate models: (a) a scavenger hunt model that familiarized students with the physical library and its collections, (b) a simulated research model where students researched random topics from a prescribed list, and (c) a course-related model where students researched a subject they were already studying in their U100 class.

Our primary concern was how to design a more effective first-year library unit. Related questions included: How can we promote student engagement? What motivates students? How do students learn, and how should this inform the way we teach library skills?

To judge the models' effectiveness, we used data from a survey administered after each library instruction session. We supplemented these survey results with comments from course instructors, student focus groups, and librarians.

Findings

A survey question asked, "Can you use library resources more effectively as a result of the library unit?" The number of students answering either "definitely yes" or "yes" was 55% for the scavenger hunt, 69% for the simulated research model, and 79% for the course-related research model.

Scavenger Hunt Model

One-minute papers and librarians' observations indicated that students participating in the scavenger hunt had some appreciation of the physical library, but little improvement in research skills. The scavenger hunt did not appear to contribute to a student's ability to use the library catalog or to begin researching a topic.

Simulated Research Model

The primary weakness of this model was poor student motivation. Focus groups revealed that students saw exercises where they had to research something from a list of random topics as irrelevant busy work because the topics were not "real." They also viewed library instruction as premature if they did not have an actual research assignment that required them to use the library.

Course-Related Research Model

We paired the library unit with the careers unit of the U100 course. Students learned library skills by researching a career of their choice. As a result, the students perceived the assignment to be relevant and real, reported higher motivation to learn library skills, and instructors reported students wrote better quality papers now than in previous library units.

Conclusions

To be effective, the library unit must teach the research skills academic classes require. This indicates the need for a research-based, not a scavenger-hunt model. Students also need to research a real-life topic or issue in order to see value in the activity. A course-related approach is more likely to satisfy these requirements.

Contact

Laura Baker
Government Documents Librarian
First-Year Library Liaison
221 Brown Library
ACU Box 29208
Abilene, TX 79699-9208
Phone: (325) 674-2477
Fax: (325) 674-2202
E-mail: bakerl@acu.edu

Appalachian State University

The Institution

Appalachian State University (ASU) is a public, regional comprehensive university that offers degrees at the baccalaureate, master's, and specialist's levels. Located in Boone, North Carolina, this four-year, residential university enrolls approximately 14,000 students, making it the sixth largest institution in the University of North Carolina system. Ninety percent of ASU students are full-time undergraduates with 50% of students living on campus or nearby. Eighty percent of Appalachian students are under the age of 22. Nearly 94% of the students are White with only 6.5% representing minorities, including 3.5% African American, 1.2% Asian American, 1.2% Hispanic, .4% Native American, and .2% non-resident alien. Appalachian has one of the higher selectivity ranks for public Southern universities with more than half of its students graduating in the top 25% of their high school class. The average SAT score of entering first-year students is 1114 and the average high school GPA is 3.65.

The Seminar

Freshman Seminar (US 1150) was first offered at Appalachian in 1987. This three-credit, graded extended orientation course is an elective that enrolls approximately 60% of the first-year class throughout the academic year. The maximum enrollment is 24 students per class. The seminar is taught by faculty members, academic advisors, student development professionals, and administrative personnel.

This course aims to acquaint students with the opportunities and demands of higher education; support them in their transition to the university; help foster cognitive and psychosocial development; broaden horizons; and assist in developing relationships with faculty, staff, and peers. Course components include study strategies, time management, personality type theory, wellness, academic computing and research, personal safety, academic integrity, diversity, the history of Appalachian State University, career planning/exploration, and cultural appreciation.

Institution Profile:
Boone, NC
Public, Four-Year
14,343
Extended Orientation
Learning Community

For the past two years, each Freshman Seminar class has been linked to another core curriculum course as part of a larger Freshman Learning Community. These learning communities bring faculty and students together to discuss, explore, and learn about a shared academic interest or common topic. The purpose of these communities is to make it easier for students to form study groups and integrate class material while making friends, meeting faculty, exploring majors, and discovering potential career choices. Examples of these Freshman Learning Communities include linking Freshman Seminar with a single core-curriculum or major-specific course such as anthropology, English, geography, mathematics, or psychology. Instructors of these communities meet often to discuss student successes and concerns, course assignments, and possible connecting points between the classes. Appalachian offers a number of learning communities reflecting the various interests of its students.

Research Design

Two studies conducted over the past several years are reported. The first highlights the benefits attributed to faculty as a result of teaching the seminar and the second explains the psychosocial gains made by seminar students as measured by the Student Development Task and Lifestyle Assessment (SDTLA) (Winston, Miller, & Cooper, 1999).

Research Design for Study 1: Freshman Seminar Faculty[1]

To determine the impact teaching the seminar had on faculty, a survey was distributed to all instructors who taught this course in the fall 2001 semester ($N = 52$). The survey was adapted from an instrument created by Fidler, Rotholz, and Richardson (1999) and was converted to a five-point Likert scale in order to ascertain strength of responses. Thirty-nine faculty members responded, yielding a return rate of 75%. While many staff personnel and administrators taught this course, only those who had teaching duties in other departments were included in the following analyses ($n = 28$).

Findings for Study 1

The data from this study illustrated four benefits associated with teaching the seminar: (a) improved teaching and the development of new pedagogical styles and techniques that can be applied to discipline-based courses, (b) better understanding of students, (c) increased knowledge about the university and its resources, and (d) increased vitality and collegiality. Table 1 highlights the quantitative results of this study.

Table 1

Effects of Teaching Freshman Seminar (US 1150) on Teaching Practices, Understanding of Students, Faculty Development, and Knowledge of Campus Resources (n = 28)

	n	Mean	% Agree or strongly agree
As a result of teaching Freshman Seminar, I…			
…am more sensitive to and understand-ing of students academic needs	28	4.46	92.9
…have a greater understanding of the variety of student services	28	4.54	92.9
…feel engaged in my work	27	4.26	92.6
…met new colleagues outside my discipline	26	4.42	92.3
…feel more committed to instructional excellence	27	4.19	88.9
…am more sensitive to and understanding of students non-academic needs	28	4.50	85.7
…feel more committed to undergraduate students as a whole	26	4.38	84.6
…use a wider variety of teaching strategies	26	4.29	82.1
…feel more a part of the university community	27	4.04	77.8
…lecture less and facilitate discussion more	26	4.19	76.9
…view my responsibilities from a wider perspective	25	4.16	76.0
…am more confident and comfortable regarding my teaching skills	28	4.04	75.0
…relate to undergraduates differently than before	26	3.88	73.1
…enjoy teaching more than before	26	4.00	73.1
…modified the content of my course syllabi in my discipline	23	3.83	65.2
…don't do anything differently	24	1.79	0.0

Research Design for Study 2: Psychosocial Development Attributed to Freshman Seminar Enrollment[2]

This study compared the psychosocial development of students enrolled in Freshman Seminar with those who were not enrolled. Students completed the Student Developmental Task and Lifestyle Assessment (Winston et al., 1999) at the beginning of their first semester in 2002 and at the beginning of their second semester in 2003. Approximately half (52%) of the 1,465 students who completed the instrument at pre- and post-test were enrolled in the seminar during the fall semester. A MANCOVA was conducted to determine if there were significant differences in subtask and subscale scores on the SDTLA due to enrollment in Freshman Seminar. Gender, minority status, and SDTLA pre-test scores were control variables in the analysis.

Findings for Study 2

Students who enrolled in Freshman Seminar reported significantly higher gains between the pre- and post-tests on the career planning, lifestyle planning, and instrumental autonomy subscales. An explanation of these subscales is below. Table 2 depicts the results of this analysis. No significant differences were found on the other nine scales.

Table 2

Adjusted SDTLA Mean Scores for Students Enrolled and Not Enrolled in Freshman Seminar

SDTLA subtask/subscale	Not enrolled	Freshman seminar
Career planning	2.55	2.62
Lifestyle planning	3.15	3.22
Instrumental autonomy	3.39	3.48

$p < .05$

The Career Planning Subtask represents students' knowledge about themselves and the world of work that enables them to make a commitment to a chosen field and formulate vocational plans. It involves taking the initial steps to prepare for employment and beginning a job search or enrollment in graduate school.

The Lifestyle Planning Subtask measures personal direction and orientation in one's life and takes into account personal, ethical, and religious values, future relationship/family plans, and vocational and educational objectives.

The Instrumental Autonomy Subtask represents students' ability to structure their lives and manipulate their environment in ways that allow them to satisfy daily needs and meet responsibilities without extensive direction or support from others. Students who have completed this subtask are able to manage their time and other aspects of their lives, establish and follow through on realistic plans, and solve most problems as they arise. They are independent, goal-directed, resourceful, and self-sufficient persons.

Notes

[1]Study conducted by Dan Friedman and Beth Glass.
[2]Study conducted by Tina Hogan, Assistant Director, Student Life and Learning Research.

References

Fidler, P., Rotholz, J., & Richardson, S. (1999). Teaching the freshman seminar: Its effectiveness in promoting faculty development. *Journal of The First-Year Experience and Students in Transition, 11*(2), 59-73.

Winston, R. B., Miller, T. K., & Cooper, D. L. (1999). *Preliminary technical manual for the Student Developmental Task and Lifestyle Assessment.* Athens, GA: Student Development Associates.

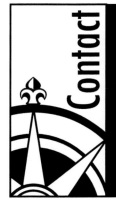

Contact

Dan Friedman
Director, Freshman Seminar & SummerPreview
Appalachian State University
Boone, NC 28607
Phone: (828) 262-2028
E-mail: friedmandb@appstate.edu

Bristol Community College

The Institution

Bristol Community College, located in Fall River, Massachusetts, is a comprehensive two-year public, commuter college offering more than 90 career and transfer programs leading to associate degrees or certificates. Annually enrolling more than 6,000 students in credit-bearing classes, BCC is ethnically and linguistically diverse. Students from 25 countries attend BCC. Approximately 61% of students are first-generation college students, with neither parent possessing a four-year degree. Fifty-one percent (51%) percent of BCC's students are over age 21; 81.6% are White; 5% are African American, Non-Hispanic; 2.8% are Hispanic; and 1.5% are Asian.

The Seminar

Bristol Community College's first-year seminar, *College Success Seminar* (CSS), was developed as part of a federal, Title III/HEA grant, Strengthening Developing Institutions, during the 2000-2001 academic year. The course carries one credit and is limited to 20 students per section. Learning is viewed as an active process based on class discussion, readings, projects, and lectures. Faculty, student affairs staff, and administrators, including BCC's president, teach CSS. Enrollment in the seminar grew 30% from fall 2001 to fall 2002 and 34% from fall 2002 to fall 2003. In existence for three years, CSS enrolls 35% of first-year students annually.

Sections are geared toward different academic and social needs, although developing an appreciation of the world of work and lifelong learning are key learning objectives. The stand-alone CSS is a discipline-based extended orientation seminar that addresses academic and survival skills such as critical thinking, study skills, and orientation to the values of higher education. CSS learning community sections include business, computer science, health science, and human services and are discipline-specific models. For example, CSS for business majors includes linked accounting and English courses and explores different aspects of business. In

Institution Profile:
Fall River, MA
Public, Two-Year
6,639
Hybrid
Learning Community

the section for culinary arts, students focus on communication and negotiation in a fast-paced environment.

Research Design

The Institutional Research (IR) Office maintains historical data files on all students at the College. Demographic information, course enrollment history, and student data such as retention and grade point average (GPA) are included in the files. This study compares retention rates and GPAs of students enrolled in CSS with a similar group of first-year students who were not enrolled in CSS. In addition, at the end of each semester, the IR office conducts a student satisfaction questionnaire of all students enrolled in CSS. Survey data are merged with historical data.

This study focuses on data collected for two fall semesters—fall 2001, the first semester that CSS was offered and fall 2003, the most recent fall semester. Retention and GPA are measured in the subsequent spring semesters—spring 2002 and spring 2004 for CSS participants and non-participants.

Findings

Many of BCC's students are academically at-risk, low-income, and first-generation college students. CSS helps students adjust socially and academically to college and develop an awareness of college expectations, values, and resources. Survey results in 2001 indicate that 98% of students reported that they practiced college study skills in CSS and used them in other classes. Ninety-four percent began to understand college expectations, and 97% began to examine career goals. More than 62% used the tutoring center or other academic support center at least once, and 75% used the Internet or an online database for research.

In fall 2002, sections were added for students who were unsure of their majors, academically at-risk, on probation, or first-generation. These students, whose reading and writing scores were below college level, reported high rates of satisfaction in their adjustment to college. Students reported in 2003 that they gained confidence in asking for help (89%), became acquainted with students whose backgrounds were different from their own (78%), and began to understand the general education curriculum (94%). Despite the many high-risk students enrolled in CSS, the 2003 cohort returned at a statistically significant higher rate (86%) than those students who did not take CSS (75%, $p < .05$).

CSS continues to grow and develop. In fall 2003, discipline-specific sections were added for health sciences and human services to help students prepare for the rigorous academic work ahead. A CSS section linked to psychology created a CSS learning community. In 2003, statistically significant differences in GPAs were found between the engineering transfer students who took the seminar and those who did not ($p < .05$). This discipline was the only one that demonstrated a statistically significant improvement in GPAs for students who took CSS. Additional CSS learning communities were added in fall 2004, including those for English, business, and computer information systems.

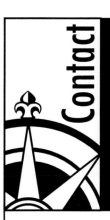

Contact

Randi Korn
Retention Coordinator, QUEST Program/ First Year Seminar Coordinator
Bristol Community College
777 Elsbree Street
Fall River, MA 02720
Phone: (508) 678-2811, ext. 2660
Fax: (508) 675-2294
E-mail: rkorn@bristol.mass.edu

Additional Contributor:

Rhonda Gabovitch
Dean of Institutional Research, Planning, and Assessment

Bryant University

The Institution

Bryant University (formerly Bryant College), founded in 1863, is a private, independent college located in Smithfield, Rhode Island, 12 miles northwest of Providence. Bryant is a four-year coeducational institution with 2,889 full-time and 247 part-time undergraduates. In 2003, Bryant undergraduates came from 31 states and 31 countries. Most students are residential with only 16% of the population commuting. The undergraduate student body is 60% male and 40% female. The entering first-year students in fall 2003 were 56% male and 44% female. Of those students, 87% were White, 7% were minorities (i.e., 2.4% Hispanic, 1.9% African American, 1.5% Asian/Pacific Islander, 0.3% Native American, and 1.1% other), 1% were non-resident aliens, and 5% did not report their ethnicity.

The Seminar

Bryant's first-year seminar is entitled *Foundations for Learning* (FFL). Bryant has had some type of non-credit, first-year seminar for eight years. The first was a non-credit, extended orientation program called "Avenues to Success in College," designed as a retention initiative. Two years later, another first-year seminar was implemented. This iteration, the "First-Year Success Program," attempted to aid retention by including a wider representation of college faculty and staff instructors. This non-credit course was mandatory for students, but students could drop out at any time without repercussions. Student life and academics were the main content. The most recent iteration, FFL, has only been in existence for two years as a required, one-credit course for *all* full-time, first-year students. FFL is an academic seminar with generally uniform content across sections and attempts to provide, as requested by faculty, a more academically rigorous experience for students. Students are required to take the course during their first semester. Approximately 40 sections are offered with a maximum enrollment of 20 students per section. Typically, tenure-track faculty teach one third of the sections, and a combination of academic and student affairs administrators teach the remaining sections.

Institution Profile:

Smithfield, RI

Private, Four-Year

3,459

Academic w/Uniform

Content

This course is designed to help first-year students become engaged members of the Bryant academic community. The course encourages students to take responsibility for their education by focusing on the process of learning how to learn and cultivating the habits of mind necessary for lifelong achievement and success. Students are encouraged to link critical thinking with writing and discussion from intellectual, social, and emotional perspectives. Students are asked to reflect on their past, present, and future in an effort to develop their own perspectives on learning and success.

The primary course goals focus on helping students to take responsibility for their education by:

- Understanding the importance of being actively involved in the educational process
- Developing cognitive and metacognitive abilities
- Developing a fuller understanding of a range of learning and study strategies
- Learning how planning and prioritizing impact academic success
- Developing self-concept including an awareness of health and wellness issues
- Developing communication skills including those related to collaboration and leadership
- Engaging in scholarly activities such as group discussion, conducting research, and synthesizing materials
- Understanding the importance of respecting diversity as a member of the Bryant community and as a citizen of the world

Research Design

Three self-report surveys were conducted and Student Instructional Report (SIR) II data were collected during the fall 2003 semester. Further, a focus group was conducted during the spring 2004 semester to gauge faculty and student perceptions of FFL. For brevity's sake, the focus here is on the end-of-semester student survey. The goal of the assessment was to determine whether curriculum changes implemented in fall 2003 were working toward achieving course goals. Students responded to eight Likert-scale questions and two open-ended questions. The Likert-scale questions corresponded to the course goals; students indicated the extent to which the course met each goal. The open-ended questions asked students to consider what they would or would not change about FFL and what advice they would give next year's incoming students regarding college and/or FFL.

Findings

Self-Report Survey Data

Students were generally positive when asked whether FFL course objectives were met. Table 1 summarizes their responses. Students seemed to feel most strongly that the course had helped them learn that planning and prioritizing impact academic success.

Table 1
Meeting Course Objectives (N = 627)

	SA		N		SD		M
	1	2	3	4	5	No ans.	
1. FFL has helped me understand the importance of being actively involved in my educational process.	17%	37%	25%	12%	9%		2.58
2. FFL has helped me develop my cognitive and metacognitive abilities (i.e., those skills involved in the self-regulation of learning).	9%	34%	33%	14%	10%		2.78
3. FFL has helped me develop a fuller understanding of a range of learning and study strategies.	14%	38%	26%	14%	10%	1	2.71
4. FFL has helped me learn how planning and prioritizing impact academic success.	19%	39%	23%	10%	9%	1	2.49
5. FFL has helped me develop self-concept including an awareness of health and wellness issues.	12%	28%	32%	16%	12%		2.93
6. FFL has helped me develop communication skills including those related to collaboration and leadership.	8%	25%	36%	17%	14%	1	3.03
7. FFL has helped me engage in scholarly activities such as group discussion, conducting research, and synthesizing materials.	10%	27%	34%	17%	12%		2.93
8. FFL has helped me understand the importance of respecting diversity as a member of the Bryant community and as a citizen of the world.	16%	32%	28%	14%	10%		2.75

Note. Students responded on a five-point Likert-type scale where 1 = Strongly Agree and 5 = Strongly Disagree.

Student Instructional Report (SIR) II Data

Students' responses on the Student Instructional Report (SIR) forms were generally positive. The overall mean rating course organization and planning for all 33 instructors was 4.12 on a scale of 1 to 5, with 5 being very effective. The overall mean for communication was nearly identical at 4.13. The highest mean of 4.41 was reported for faculty/student interaction, not surprising for such a course. Students rated assignments, exams, and grading a 3.89. The two remaining scores were the lowest: course outcomes at 2.79 and student effort and involvement at 2.50. These scores fell within the moderate to somewhat ineffective range.

Focus Group Data

In spring 2004, approximately 180 out of 773 first-year students participated in focus groups in an effort to assess students' overall first-year experience with the institution. The questions focused on three main areas of the students' experience: (a) academics, (b) campus culture, and (c) facilities. Responses regarding FFL were elicited during the discussions on academics.

In general, first-year students indicated that they felt challenged by the curriculum, experienced positive interactions with faculty and staff, and felt they benefited from the learning assistance programs available to them on campus. Students tended to be more critical when discussing specific courses. Feedback about FFL seemed to be mixed: Approximately half of the sample articulated that they felt the course was extremely valuable, though an equal number indicated "it did not help them."

Implications

A majority of students responded on the self-report and SIR surveys that they felt course objectives were being met. They felt, for example, that FFL had helped them be more involved in their educational process (54% agreed or strongly agreed, while 21% disagreed or strongly disagreed) and understand how planning and prioritizing impact their academic success (58% agreed or strongly agreed, while 19% disagreed or strongly disagreed).

Approximately half the participants in focus groups felt that the course was not helpful, while the written assessment showed that approximately 9% of the students felt they were not helped or supported by the course. The discrepancy in the two self-report measures could be explained by the nature of the reporting mechanisms and the difference in sample sizes. In the focus groups, students ($N = 180$) were asked for verbal feedback in front of their peers, which may have resulted in socially acceptable responses. Students may not have felt comfortable admitting the extent to which the course helped them with the transition from high school to college. On the written assessments, students (N = 627) were free to indicate their responses anonymously and perhaps felt able to be more candid as a result.

It is important to note that each mechanism used to solicit students' feedback was implemented early in their academic careers. Students may not have had the opportunity to accurately assess whether, for example, the course had helped them develop cognitive and metacognitive abilities. One indication of this is the response of neutral in the course objectives portion of the self-report survey. For each objective, between one quarter and one third of students responded "neutral," indicating that perhaps they have not had time to assess each area. More long-term surveys could supplement this early assessment in order to gauge student perception more effectively.

These findings demonstrate the importance of conducting systematic research to gauge student perceptions. Many college campuses are still in the process of introducing first-year seminars into their curricula. The tendency is to rely on anecdotal student feedback and campus musings to determine the effectiveness of these new courses. This research suggests that more rigorous assessment is critical to obtain an accurate indication of course effectiveness.

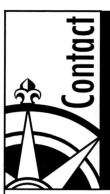

Contact

Laurie L. Hazard
Director, Academic Center for Excellence and Writing Center
Bryant University
1150 Douglas Pike
Smithfield, Rhode Island 02917
Phone: (401) 232-6746
Fax: (401) 232-6038
E-mail: lhazard@bryant.edu

Additional Contributor:
Jean-Paul Nadeau
Associate Director, Academic Center for Excellence and Writing Center

California State University, Northridge

The Institution

California State University, Northridge (CSUN) is located in the state's San Fernando Valley. Current enrollment is 24,300 full-time equivalent students; 1,900 live in on-campus housing. We are a four-year, master's degree-granting, regional comprehensive public university. In fall 2002, the average age of our undergraduate students was 24.2 years. Approximately 61% were women. Our student population is 35.9% White, 15.2% Mexican, 9.3% other Hispanic, 8.5% Asian American, 7.7% African American, 4.2% Pacific Islander (3.9% Filipino), 3.6% International, 0.6% American Indian, and 16.5% other.

Institution Profile:

Northridge, CA

Public, Four-Year

32,618

Hybrid

The Seminar

University 100 (U100), the first-year seminar, has been offered continuously at CSUN since fall 1999. It is an elective, letter-graded, baccalaureate course carrying three hours of general education credit. Though it is primarily an extended orientation seminar, U100 incorporates several units on basic study skills. The enrollment limit is 25 students per section; we typically enroll about 10% of first-time, first-year students annually. Faculty who teach the course hold at least a master's degree or equivalent. About one quarter of instructors are full-time, tenure-track faculty, while the rest are full- and part-time lecturers with considerable experience teaching first-year students.

The primary course goals (as they appear in the course syllabus) focus on helping students develop the skills and strategies necessary for excellence in academic, personal, and professional life. Ethics, time management, and information competence anchor the course content. Upon completion of the course, students should be able to:

1. Demonstrate familiarity with the history and purpose of higher education
2. Discuss the role of the university in society

3. Describe the roles, rights, and responsibilities of university students, faculty, and staff
4. Demonstrate problem-solving and goal-setting skills
5. Describe the concepts presented in the CSUN mission, values, and vision statement
6. Demonstrate familiarity with academic policies and programs and show proficiency in locating that information in the University catalog
7. Assess their strengths and weaknesses in basic academic and communication skills including reading and listening with comprehension, organizing ideas for presentation, writing brief reaction papers and reports, speaking in public, participating in group discussions, and working cooperatively in diverse communities

Research Design

With the cooperation of our campus's Office of Institutional Research, we track key performance indicators [e.g., grade point average (GPA), units earned, persistence/retention, and academic standing] longitudinally. We also participate in a formal research study conducted by a faculty member in the Educational Psychology and Counseling Department assessing college students' adaptation to university life. Data were collected during the fall 2002 and fall 2003 semesters from students enrolled in U100 and from a control group of first-year students not enrolled in U100. Each student completed the *Student Adaptation to College Questionnaire* and a demographic questionnaire in class during weeks 2 and 13 of the semester.

Findings

Results of our assessments have demonstrated three distinct student outcomes. First, U100 students show higher GPAs than their non-U100 peers. Second, U100 students outperform non-U100 peers in maintaining good academic standing (see Table 1). More important, this difference persists through several semesters. Finally, U100 students showed a stronger personal/emotional adaptation to college as compared to non-U100 students. The statistically significant difference was even maintained when students were grouped according to their academic readiness.

Table 1

Impact of U100 on First-Year Student GPA and Academic Standing

	1999 Cohort		2002 Cohort	
	Non-U100 (n = 1,018)	U100 (n= 137)	Non-U100 (n = 2,302)	U100 (n = 279)
Avg. GPA	2.73	2.79	2.65	2.74**
Good academic standing (%)	44	47	63	68**
Disqualified (%)	3	2	12	7**

**p < .01

GPAs for the 1999 and 2002 cohorts were examined in spring 2003 (that is, after eight and two semesters at CSUN, respectively). The percent of students in academic good standing (GPA 2.0 or higher) was also evaluated. For both cohorts, GPAs and the percent of students in good academic standing are higher for the U100 students than for the students who did not take U100. Statistically significant differences were found for the 2002 cohort in both GPA and academic standing. The non-significance of the differences found with the 1999 cohort may be due to the smaller sample size as a result of dropouts and transfers.

As evidenced by higher scores on the *Student Adaptation to College Questionnaire* (SACQ), U100 students experience a more successful personal-emotional adaptation to college. This research showed that "There is a small, but significant correlation among students' adaptation to college as measured by the SACQ (Baker & Siryk, 1999) and high school GPA, SAT, first-semester college GPA, and the U100 course grade" (Simon & Tovar, 2004). In addition, "higher adaptation was the predicted—and actual—outcome for those in U100" (Simon & Tovar).

Reference

Simon, M. A., & Tovar, E. (2004). Academically and ethnically diverse first-year students' adaptation to college: The effect of the first-year experience seminar. Manuscript submitted for publication.

Cheryl Spector
Director, Freshman Seminar
Professor, English Department
Undergraduate Studies, mail drop 8203
California State University, Northridge
18111 Nordhoff Street
Northridge, CA 91330-8203
Phone: (818) 677-2969
Fax: (818) 677-3977
E-mail: cheryl.spector@csun.edu

 # California State University, San Marcos

The Institution

California State University, San Marcos is a publicly funded (state-supported), four-year institution in northern San Diego County that enrolls approximately 7,200 students. The University now has one residential facility; but at the time the study was done, all students were commuters. The population of first-year students is of traditional age (17 - 19), although the median student age for all students on campus is 22. The majority of students (62.8%) are women. The largest ethnic group on campus is White (52.6%); however, there is a large Hispanic population (18.0%) as well. There is less representation from other ethnic groups with Asian/Pacific Islander being the next largest at 9.4%. African Americans represent 2.7% of the student body and Native Americans 0.8%. The remaining students indicate either "other" at 6.1% or "'No Response/Decline" at 10.0%.

The Seminar

In 1995, the first group of first-year students was introduced to Cal State San Marcos and since then the school has offered a three-credit first-year seminar course: GEL 101, *The Student, The University and the Community*. The optional course fulfills an area requirement for general education for graduation from the University.

The GEL 101 is a basic study skills first-year seminar designed to help students succeed in college. The course has traditionally been taught by either faculty or professional staff on campus, and the size of the class varies from approximately 25 to 35 students per class. A majority of students sign up for the GEL 101 course at new student orientation during the summer or winter. The course lasts the full semester (currently 16 weeks) and meets for approximately three hours each week. Topics include time management, study skills, oral presentation skills, career development, library information and research, and health and wellness. The course also includes at least one comprehensive group presentation. There are eight stated objectives for GEL 101:

Institution Profile:

San Marcos, CA

Public, Four-Year

7,783

Basic Study Skills

1. Diversity
2. Information literacy and ability to conduct college-level research
3. Retention and self-directed learning
4. Institutional awareness/resource management
5. Interpersonal relations
6. Academic and career planning
7. Well being
8. Moral and ethical decision making

Research Design

To determine the effect of GEL 101 on continuation rates, a simple computation involving percentage rates was performed. The data were separated into two groups: non-GEL students and GEL students. Percentages were then computed for the students for the end of the first semester and the end of the second semester. Because all first-year students are given the opportunity to enroll in GEL 101, the students self-select to take the course based upon whether it fits into their class schedules and whether the course has seats available. All first-year students attend a new student orientation where they register for courses. As a result, the distribution of non-GEL students and GEL students are very similar with regard to demographics, incoming SAT scores, and high school GPAs.

For the academic success portion of the study, two groups of data were compared: (a) students who did not take the GEL 101 course and (b) students who did. Only data from the second term were analyzed so that the actual grade from the GEL 101 was not a confounding factor.

Findings

Research on the course was conducted during the spring 2002 for the fall 1995 to spring 2000 semesters. The results from this study show a difference in the continuation rates and academic success of GEL 101 students versus non-GEL 101 students. The results of the analysis of continuation rates show a statistically significant difference in second semester continuation rates between GEL students and non-GEL students (Table 1). The difference in mean GPAs is statistically significant with GEL students earning 0.30 points more than non-GEL students (Table 2).

The results of the study seem to indicate that if Cal State San Marcos is concerned about the academic success and continuation rates of its first-time, first-year students, the opportunity to take the course should be extended to all new students.

Table 1

Percentage of GEL 100 and Non-GEL 100 Students Retained

	Term 1	Term 2
Non-GEL 100 students (N = 897)	87.6	66.7
All GEL 100 students (N = 1,470)	94.3	88.5

Term 1: χ^2 = 2.69; Term 2: χ^2 = 33.11

**$p < .01$

Table 2

Mean Second Term GPA for GEL 100 and Non-GEL 100 Students

	Count	Mean GPA	Variance
Non-GEL 100 students	896	2.31**	1.43
All GEL 100 students	1470	2.61**	0.99

**$p < .01$

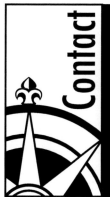

Jane Sparks
Coordinator, Freshman/Sophomore Advising
California State University, San Marcos
333 Twin Oaks Valley Road
San Marcos, CA 92096-0001
Phone: (760) 750-4072
Fax: (760) 750-4111
E-mail: jsparks@csusm.edu

Cardinal Stritch University

The Institution

Cardinal Stritch University (CSU) is a private, four-year, independent, Catholic institution sponsored by the Sisters of St. Francis of Assisi. It is located in an urban/suburban environment in Milwaukee, WI. Stritch is rooted in the liberal arts, offering associate's, bachelor's, and master's degrees with one doctoral program. Its enrollment is 4,783 full-time and 2,031 part-time undergraduate and graduate students. Stritch is mainly a commuter school with fewer than 10% traditional-age students (i.e., ages 18 - 21) living in residence halls. In the College of Arts and Sciences, 68% of the students are female. The racial makeup of the student body is approximately 76% White, 13% African American, 2% Hispanic, 2% Asian American/Pacific Islander, 1% non-resident alien, 1% Native American, and 5% unknown/not reported.

The Seminar

Previously, incoming first-year students in the College of Arts and Sciences (CAS) were required to take a college transition course called Freshman Seminar. In response to negative student assessments of the course, a new college transition experience was created. Beginning in 2000, all incoming first-year students in the CAS are required to enroll in a three-credit first-year experience (FYE) course coupled with a mandatory weeklong orientation program. The FYE course is designed to introduce students to the rigors of college academics while the orientation experience introduces students to college life.

The FYE course is a discussion-based, academic seminar with variable content with each course designed around a topic taken from a liberal arts discipline selected by the instructor. FYE instructors are full-time faculty who teach their course as part of their normal load or as an overload. Each FYE course starts during orientation week and ends a month early so that students have one less course to manage at the end of the semester. Each course has an enrollment of 15 to 18 students and includes the following common objectives:

Institution Profile:

Milwaukee, WI

Private, Four-Year

6,785

Hybrid

- Development of critical-thinking skills
- Development of communication skills
- Understanding of the role of the liberal arts in students' personal and professional lives
- Mastery of course-specific outcomes as determined by the instructor

Instructors also address plagiarism, note-taking and study skills, test-taking strategies, classroom behavior, and how to interact with faculty. In addition, all FYE courses must include a written test, a writing assignment, and an oral presentation.

The second component of the FYE program is a weeklong, mandatory orientation. Students earn credit for their FYE course by attending orientation. Primary goals of new student orientation are to acquaint new students and their families with the mission, programs, and services of the University, educate students of their rights and responsibilities within the campus and the community, and emphasize the importance of being involved on campus. Orientation helps students feel confident, connected to the Stritch community, and excited about their college choice. During orientation, students

- Become oriented to campus resources and facilities
- Learn about campus rules, regulations, and policies
- Are introduced to alcohol and drug education, sexual assault issues, library and computer use, and time management

Research Design

Assessment of the FYE course includes a pre-course survey exploring student attitudes about college life, a post-course survey assessing those same attitudes while also determining if their FYE course met program objectives, and an instructor focus group. In 2003, students also completed the First-Year Initiative (FYI) Assessment. In addition, all instructors are required to have students complete a mandatory, University-designed instructor evaluation. We currently have three years of assessment data.

Findings

In response to negative attitudes about Stritch's first college transition course, a new type of FYE course was developed. Students consider the new FYE course a valuable experience: On a scale of 1 "not at all" to 5 "a great deal," the mean response (MR) was 4.2. This finding was further substantiated when students were asked to respond in writing to the question: "What would you change about your FYE course if you could?" The most common response was "nothing" (38%), and only 3% of the students suggested that the course not be required.

As shown in Table 1, 62% of students felt their FYE course either improved or greatly improved their understanding of the value of a liberal arts education. Fifty-eight percent felt their FYE course improved or greatly improved their ability to express themselves through writing, but this area needs improvement. The most positive responses came with questions dealing with critical thinking.

Table 1
Course Outcomes Resulting From FYE Enrollment

Percentage of those responding that FYE has improved or greatly improved. . .	2001 (n = 86)	2002 (n = 73)	2003 (n = 71)	Average
Your understanding of the value of a liberal arts education	73	56	58	62
What is meant by a liberal arts education	71	61	55	62
Your ability to write clearly[1]	47	74	53	58
Your ability to present an argument and a counter-argument	71	68	68	69
Your depth of thinking about important issues	75	77	76	76

[1]From the 2003 First-Year Initiative (FYI) Assessment.

As part of the transition into college life, students need to become comfortable with their university, their instructors, and their peers. One of the goals of the FYE course is to help students make that transition to college life. Results indicate that students feel their FYE course has helped with their adjustment to college life, their interactions with faculty, their confidence that they will succeed, their feeling of comfort at Stritch, and their getting to know other students (See Table 2).

Table 2

Survey Results for Questions Dealing With Adjustments to College Life

Percentage of those responding that FYE has improved or greatly improved. . .	2001 (n = 86)	2002 (n = 73)	2003 (n = 71)	Average
Your getting to know other students[1]	86	85	84	85
Your interactions with faculty	56	63	77	65
Your confidence that you will succeed at CSU	77	74	68	73
Your adjustment to college life	72	78	67	72
Your level of comfort at CSU	72	74	76	74

[1]From the 2003 First-Year Initiative (FYI) Assessment.

Conclusion

Each FYE course is unique. Although every FYE instructor develops his or her course using FYE guidelines, how he or she chooses to meet the common course objectives is up to the individual instructor. When assessment data are sorted by section, mean responses do vary among sections, sometimes by as much as a full point. Some variability is expected because each course is different. For example, the FYE course *Writing Your Own Story* is writing intensive and, therefore, student responses to questions asking if their FYE course improved writing skills are always much higher than other sections. The instructor for the FYE course *Genetic Engineering: The New Frankenstein?* stresses understanding the value of the liberal arts and requires that students do a specific project on this topic. This class always garners very high mean responses to questions concerning the value of a liberal arts education. The genetic engineering section was offered in 2001, but not in 2002 and 2003. The inclusion of a discipline-specific section could explain the decrease in percentages of those responding that their FYE section had improved or greatly improved their understanding of the value of a liberal arts education (See Table 1). Because FYE courses are not exactly the same and because the slate of FYE courses offered from year to year changes, some variation in assessment data will occur.

Another possible explanation for decreases in mean responses observed in 2003 could be attributed to an FYE section that received uncharacteristically poor marks on the post-course survey. This FYE course and its instructor have always received very high marks on assessment surveys. However, in 2003, student responses to survey questions in this section were unusually negative overall. Two things distinguished this section from other sections taught in 2003. First, the instructor changed the format from a 1-hour-and-20-minute format meeting twice a week to a format that met for three hours one day per week. In free response questions, most students indicated extreme displeasure at the way the course was scheduled. In addition, this course had an unusually high enrollment of more than 20 students. The negative attitudes caused by how often the class met coupled with the difficulty of running a discussion-based course with so many students could have carried over into unenthusiastic responses to survey questions. Because this section had such a high enrollment, the negative responses may have affected assessment data by causing the slight decrease in scores observed in 2003.

The variability in survey responses between sections is of concern. To address this problem, assessment data are shared with FYE instructors at the end of the year, and large differences in student responses between sections are discussed. In addition, a FYE instructor workshop was offered for the first time in the spring of 2004. A portion of the workshop re-emphasizes the need for faculty to address all topics and activities common to FYE courses as identified in the general course guidelines.

Contact

Debra Meuler
Assistant Professor, Department of Natural Sciences
Program Coordinator, First Year Experience Program
Cardinal Stritch University
6801 N. Yates Road
Milwaukee, WI 53217
Phone: (414) 410-4136
E-mail: dameuler@stritch.edu

Additional Contributors:
Connie Borowicz
Associate Dean of Students

Margaret Wilhite
Assistant Professor, Department of Sociology

Eastern Connecticut State University

The Institution

Eastern Connecticut State University (ECSU) is located in Willimantic, Connecticut. It is a four-year, public liberal arts institution, enrolling 3,700 full-time undergraduates and 5,156 students total in fall 2004. Approximately 2,200 undergraduates reside on campus. The student body is 58% female. Eastern's undergraduate ethnic enrollment is as follows: White 82.4%, African American 7.0%, Hispanic 4.1%, Asian American 1.4%, Native American 0.8%, non-resident alien 0.8%, and other/unknown 3.6%. Approximately 51% of ECSU's students are first-generation students (i.e., their parents do not hold college degrees).

The Seminar

The first-year seminar, called *Resources, Research, and Responsibilities*, is a key component of ECSU's First-Year Program. It is an extended orientation course similar to the University of South Carolina's University 101 seminar and continues for the duration of the fall term. The seminar is required for First-Year Program participants, but enrollment in the First-Year Program is voluntary. The seminar is a one-credit course with a maximum enrollment of 25 students. A full-time, tenured or tenure-track faculty member teaches the seminar. In fall 2004, 13 sections enrolled approximately 37% of all first-time, first-year students.

The primary course goals are to show students how to improve their academic skills, make the best use of ECSU's library and computer resources, manage their time and stress, and generally make an effective adjustment to college. All First-Year Program (FYP) participants register for a "cluster" of three classes. The cluster includes two three-credit courses that meet part of the students' general education requirements (GER) and the one-credit seminar. The students, faculty members, and peer mentors (students from previous years of the FYP who assist in the seminar) compose a "learning community."

Research Design

Evaluation of the FYP was conducted using two methods. First, we computed the percentage of seminar students retained for one year, as compared to those who did not participate in the FYP. We also administered a survey to all FYP students during the final week of the seminar in fall 2002 and fall 2003. Survey respondents indicated their level of agreement with each of 34 items (fall 2002 survey) or 45 items (fall 2003 survey) on the following scale: Strongly Disagree, Disagree, Neither Agree nor Disagree, Agree, Strongly Agree. The percentages of respondents who answered "Agree" or "Strongly Agree" (i.e., "Percent Favorable") for selected items are presented in the table below.

The first section of each survey asked respondents about the FYP in general. The second section asked students about possible changes to the program. A third section asked about the enhancement of abilities related to college success (e.g., oral communication, researching a topic, time management), and a final section presented respondents with open-ended questions.

Findings

The FYP has had a positive impact on retention. Four of the five FYP cohorts have exceeded the non-FYP first-time, first-year student cohort in terms of one-year retention by at least 7% (see Table 1). The fall 2000 class did not surpass its comparison group. A chi-square test was conducted for each first-year student cohort to assess the statistical impact of the FYP on retention. Cohorts marked with an asterisk have statistically significant differences ($p < .05$).

Table 1
FYP Impact on Retention for 1999-2003 Cohorts

Cohort	FYP participants	Percent retained	Non-FYP participants	Percent retained
Fall 1999*	150	77	252	69
Fall 2000	69	74	754	74
Fall 2001*	146	82	686	75
Fall 2002*	206	82	598	72
Fall 2003*	263	81	513	72

*$p < .05$

A survey of FYP participants indicated that they were generally satisfied with their experience in the program (see Table 2). Participants indicated the following:

- They enjoyed participation and would recommend the program to incoming first-year students (items 1 and 2).
- FYP was beneficial in terms of adjusting to college life (item 3).
- They were more ambivalent about other potential benefits of the program: becoming involved in the ECSU community (item 4), deciding what courses to take (item 5), making decisions about one's college career (item 6), and developing new academic skills (item 7).
- The "learning community" aspect of the FYP worked well (items 8 and 9).
- Some respondents felt that the FYP gave them certain advantages over non-FYP students. This was particularly true in the area of knowing about all the resources available to students at ECSU (items 10-13).

Table 2

Survey Items Indicating Satisfaction Among FYP Participants

	Survey item	Percent favorable 2002	Percent favorable 2003
1.	I would recommend the Blue Sky Program to incoming first-year students at ECSU.	67	73
2.	I enjoyed participating in the Blue Sky Program.	73	67
3.	I feel that the Blue Sky Program has helped me to adjust to college life.	59	62
4.	Participating in the Blue Sky Program has helped me to become involved in the ECSU community.	27	37
5.	Participating in the Blue Sky Program has helped me decide what courses to take next semester.	32	37
6.	Participating in the Blue Sky Program has helped me to make long-term decisions about my college career.	30	36
7.	The FYR course helped me develop new academic skills.	35	35
8.	Spending a lot of time in class with the same group of students encouraged me to interact with them.	75	77
9.	Working with peers helped me become a better student.	53	47
10.	Compared to my friends at ECSU who are not in the Blue Sky Program, I think that I have had an easier time adjusting to college life.	36	—
11.	Compared to my friends at ECSU who are not in the Blue Sky Program, I like my courses better.	36	—
12.	I think that I know more about the resources available at ECSU than my friends who are not in the Blue Sky Program.	60	—
13.	I think that I feel more positive about my first semester at ECSU than my friends who are not in the Blue Sky Program.	33	—

Note. "Blue Sky Program" is former name of FYP. "FYR course" refers to the First-Year Seminar.

At the end of fall 2002, students were asked about whether certain changes or adjustments should be made to the FYP in future years. The percentage of respondents who answered "Agree" or "Strongly Agree" is represented in the recommendations below.

- One third (33%) favored eliminating the first-year seminar, whereas 44% did not.
- Some students would recommend increasing the first-year seminar course to two or three credits (28% and 14%, respectively). However, the majority were against increasing the credits to two or three (59% and 72%, respectively).
- A majority of students (76%) would have liked a course from their major area included in their cluster.

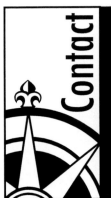

Brian Lashley
Assistant Director of Institutional Research
Gelsi-Young Hall
Eastern Connecticut State University
83 Windham St.
Willimantic, CT 06226
Phone: (860) 465-5306
Fax: (860) 465-5083

Endicott College

The Institution

Endicott College, located in Beverly, Massachusetts, is on New England's historic North Shore, 20 miles north of Boston. Endicott College's approach to the first year has evolved over the past 15 years as the college moved from a private, two-year women's college (enrollment 550) to a private, coeducational institution granting bachelor's and master's degrees (enrollment 1,600 undergraduates). In the fall of 2003, there were 484 first-year students, all traditional age (18 - 22). Ninety-seven percent lived on campus, 65% were female, 89% were White, 3.5% were non-resident aliens and 2.6% were of ethnic origin (African American, Hispanic, Asian, or Native American). Eighteen percent of the first-year students were first-generation college students based on data obtained from the 2003 National Survey of Student Engagement (NSSE).

The Seminar

At Endicott College, we recognize that no two students experience college in the same way or at the same pace. Yet we are dedicated to creating common threads to run through the fabric of the "Endicott experience," anticipating increased self-confidence, stronger professional skills, technological competencies and, perhaps most valuable, lives open to change. This begins with our first-year seminar (LA100), required of all first-year students since the fall of 2001. The seminar is a three-credit academic seminar with variable content designed to introduce students to inquiry-based learning skills that provide the foundation for their four years of study at Endicott College. Class size is limited to 20 students. Faculty members choose themes reflective of their interests within their field and incorporate this content to address the learning objectives of the course. All first-time, first-year students take the course during the fall semester and are given a choice of themes.

The primary objectives of LA100 are to develop information literacy, critical reading, and inquiry skills necessary to be a liberally

Institution Profile:

Beverly, MA

Private, Four-Year

3,100

Academic w/Variable

Content

educated and successful college learner. An equally important objective of this course is to provide a close mentoring relationship between the faculty member and the student. The third major component is to instill a sense of enthusiasm and internal motivation for the love of learning and discovery. Approximately half of the faculty who teach LA100 are full-time and include faculty from all schools. Academic administrators also teach the course.

Research Design

The seminar is carefully and systematically assessed each semester. Students are given a questionnaire both at midterm and during the final exam period. The questionnaire, designed by the LA100 faculty, is a combination of Likert-scaled and open-ended questions designed to assess students understanding of the course objectives and the benefits and weaknesses of the course. Students also fill out faculty evaluations that assess both the teacher and the course. Classroom observations are conducted on a regular basis by the Assistant Dean of Arts and Sciences. In addition, first-year students take the NSSE each spring. LA100 faculty meet in the fall and spring to review student feedback and make modifications to next fall's course. Additionally, the College was selected to participate in the Foundations of Excellence® in the First College Year project sponsored by the Policy Center on the First Year of College. Numerous forms of assessment resulted including an intensive self-study of the first-year experience and two site visits by the Policy Center staff.

Findings

Since the seminar's implementation in fall 2001, the College's retention rate has increased from 69% to 80%. Results of the LA100 student surveys indicate that in 2003, 85% of the students rated the first-year seminar a positive experience, with 93% saying that the course goals were met (see Tables 1 and 2, respectively). Students feel the course helped them develop skills in writing, research, critical thinking, time management, and reading. Additionally, they stated that the course helped them acclimate to college (see Table 3).

Table 1
Students' Overall Experience in First-Year Seminar

	2002 ($n = 150$)	2003 ($n = 264$)
Positive	80%	85%
Negative	15%	11%
No opinion	5%	4%

Table 2
Students' Perception of Course Goal Attainment in First-Year Seminar

Course goals met	2002 (*n* = 150)	2003 (*n* = 264)
Yes	95%	93%
Somewhat	0%	2%
No	5%	5%

Table 3
Student-Reported Learning in First-Year Seminar

Course topics	2002 (*n* = 150)	2003 (*n* = 264)
How to acclimate to college academic life	100%	100%
Writing skills	100%	100%
Research skills	98%	98%
Critical thinking	98%	98%
Time-management skills	95%	95%
Reading skills	92%	92%

Each year, the College reflects on the results of the NSSE. In comparing 2001 to 2003 results, first-year students report an increase in memorizing, analyzing, synthesizing, making judgments, and making applications. Students also indicate an increase in the number of course readings and readings for personal enrichment. We believe the implementation of a comprehensive first-year experience program has also contributed to the changes in the NSSE results. This program includes housing first-year students in designated first-year buildings, creating out-of-class activities specifically for entering students, providing unique tutoring options, and creating a triage team of academic and student affairs personnel who help identify both the students who are struggling in their first year and the students who are demonstrating leadership skills. In spite of these interventions, NSSE results indicate that the College needs to continue to develop academic, intellectual, and social experiences as well as educational and personal growth opportunities to further student engagement.

Focus groups of LA100 students, campus visits, and student surveys have all indicated that consistency across the LA100 sections needs improvement.

To address this issue, faculty have been refining course objectives as well as developing primary reading requirements, grading rubrics, and assessment methods to be used across all sections for fall 2004. We recognize that this unique course is a work in progress and that it must constantly be evaluated and allowed to evolve.

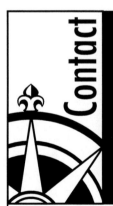

Contact

Beverly Dolinsky
Dean of Arts and Sciences
Endicott College
376 Hale Street
Beverly, MA 01915
Phone: (978) 232-2194
E-mail: bdolinsk@endicott.edu

Additional Contributor:
Kathleen Barnes
Assistant Dean of Arts and Sciences

Gallaudet University

The Institution

Gallaudet University in Washington, DC, is the world's only liberal arts university for deaf and hard of hearing students. Founded in 1864 by an Act of Congress, its charter was signed by President Abraham Lincoln. Enrollment is approximately 2,000 undergraduate and graduate students. Approximately 35% of the student population are from diverse racial and ethnic backgrounds, including 12% African American, 9% Hispanic, 6% Asian, and 2% Native American. An additional 6% of the students are international. Fifty-three percent of the students are female. Deaf and hard of hearing undergraduate students choose from more than 40 majors leading to a bachelor of arts or a bachelor of science degree. The Graduate School offers master's and doctoral-level programs. The campus also houses the Laurent Clerc National Deaf Education Center, which includes the Kendall Demonstration Elementary School and the Model Secondary School for the Deaf.

The Course

CAP 101, First-Year Seminar (FYS), is a three-credit, required course for new students, which has been offered since 1995. Enrollment is limited to 15 students per section. Instructors include faculty from a variety of academic departments as well as student affairs and academic professional staff members. An upperclass student, who enrolls in a three-credit course for teaching assistants, assists each instructor. Many sections are taught within learning communities with linked courses. Special sections include those for honors students, developmental students, and transfer students.

The primary goals of the course are to actively promote student academic success and to help students develop a lasting connection to Gallaudet. While it includes some aspects of an academic seminar, the course is primarily an extended orientation model. The curriculum includes many aspects of adjusting to college, understanding and using university resources, and exploring

Institution Profile:

Washington, DC

Public, Four-Year

1,812

Hybrid

Learning Community

majors and careers, all while developing technology, reading, writing, and critical-thinking skills.

Research Design

Before the fall of 2002, FYS was not required. From 1996 to 2001, the retention rate of students who took FYS averaged 11% higher than those who did not. When FYS became required in 2002 and comparison groups were no longer possible, assessment of FYS changed. Three assessment measures have been used:

1. An in-house instrument was developed using a 5-point Likert scale that asked students to rate their abilities and behaviors as a result of taking FYS.
2. FYS grades for students placed on academic warning after their first semester were examined to see if a correlation existed between the seminar grade and warning status.
3. Gallaudet participated in the First-Year Initiative (FYI) Assessment, a national benchmarking study that compares student feedback on first-year seminars among a group of participating institutions.

Findings

Results of the in-house FYS course assessment show that in 2003, 73% of the students indicated FYS helped them to become better Gallaudet students, and 72% would recommend the course to next year's students (Table 1). Seventy-nine percent indicated that the course made it easier for them to use campus resources.

Table 1
Course Outcomes Over a Three-Year Period

Outcome	2001 (N = 183)	2002 (N = 210)	2003 (N = 186)
Course helped me improve as a student	68%	67%	73%
Would recommend course	65%	65%	72%
Course improved campus resource use	74%	76%	79%

During the 2001-2002 academic year, FYS grades of students placed on academic warning were examined. Of the students placed on academic warning (N = 85), 60 students (70%) had either D or F grades in FYS indicating a strong correlation between grades in FYS and academic success.

First-Year Initiative (FYI) Assessment comparison information (Table 2) indicated that students rated their FYS course highly in factors associated with academic and cognitive skills and knowledge of wellness when compared to six self-selected institutions in the same Carnegie classification. Although students rated the factor labeled "sense of belonging and acceptance" relatively high, it was slightly lower than the mean of our six selected institutions.

Table 2
Gallaudet FYI Assessment Average on Selected Factors

Factors	Gallaudet		Selected 6	
	Mean	Std. Dev.	Mean	Std. Dev
Academic and cognitive skills	4.67	1.60	3.84	1.61
Knowledge of wellness	4.74	1.88	3.78	1.67
Sense of belonging and acceptance	5.28	1.59	5.42	1.36

Note. Comparison based on a sample size of six self-selected universities with similar characteristics. From *"EBI First-Year Initiative Study,"* 2003. Copyright 2004 by EBI. Adapted with permission of the author.

Conclusion

Based on the results of the three tools used to measure the effectiveness of the first-year seminar course at Gallaudet University, it appears that FYS helps a large number of students succeed during their first year. However, while students' perception of their improved academic and cognitive skills and their knowledge of wellness was high, the social/emotional aspect of the first year appears to be critical to any subsequent improvement in retention. One might speculate that students in unique universities such as Gallaudet would have no difficulty feeling that they belong. Because students come to Gallaudet from all over the country and because the world provides challenges that go beyond hearing status, the factor "sense of belonging and acceptance" may be lower than expected. Also, given that American Sign Language (ASL) is the language of instruction and interaction, students who are new to this language may initially have difficulty connecting. The factor "sense of belonging and acceptance" (which includes questions about feeling accepted, making new friends, and identifying with other students) should be targeted and analyzed in an effort to increase student retention.

Contact

Catherine Andersen
Program Director
First Year Experience
Gallaudet University
800 Florida Avenue NE
Washington, DC 20002
Phone: (202) 651-5804
E-mail: catherine.andersen@gallaudet.edu

Additional Contributors:
Judith Termini
Associate Professor

Maria Waters
Associate Professor

Indiana State University

The Institution

Indiana State University (ISU) is a four-year public university with more than 11,000 students. Located in Terre Haute, Indiana, ISU serves a largely traditional first-year population with 98% of incoming first-year students having graduated from high school in the previous 18 months. Sixty percent of our first-year students come from families in which neither parent completed a four-year degree; 40% from families in which neither parent attended a post-secondary school. The undergraduate student population is 49% male, 82.7% White, 11.4% African American, and 1.8% international, with 2% coming from other unknown backgrounds. The majority of the students come from within 75 miles of Terre Haute, and 45% live on campus.

Institution Profile:

Terre Haute, IN

Public, Four-Year

11,360

Hybrid

Learning Community

The Seminar

Indiana State University has not one, but seven distinct first-year academic seminars offered in three of the University's six colleges. These seminars, typically taught by tenure-track faculty, are required parts of the majors within these colleges and carry either one or two credit hours. College-specific courses are in addition to the Student Academic Services Center's (SASC) University 101. University 101 began at ISU in 1995 as a means to teach student athletes NCAA rules. The course has evolved to a required course in the Academic Opportunity Program (ISU's program for conditionally admitted students) and the Open Preference Program (ISU's program for undeclared students).

Each of the colleges' seminars are staffed and funded within the specific college. University 101 sections designed for students in the Academic Opportunity Program are staffed by professionals who work in the SASC, and the sections designed for Open Preference students are staffed by tenure-track faculty. University 101 is an extended orientation course, but seminars within a specific discipline are primarily introductions to a major field. Study skills, time management, and behavioral advice are addressed in all seminars to help students succeed at ISU and within their specific college. Table 1 outlines the various first-year seminars, their student populations, course titles, descriptions, goals for each of the seminars, and the degree to which seminar sections are part of learning communities. The majority of the first-year seminars are tied to learning communities designed for specific majors (e.g., business, technology, nursing).

Research Design

The most recently conducted study uses a logistic and linear regression to explore the impact of first-year seminars embedded in learning communities versus stand-alone seminars on retention and first-semester grade point average (GPA). This analysis held constant the pre-entry variables of high school diploma type, high school GPA, high school rank, SAT, first-generation status, family income, gender, race, and the programmatic participation variable for learning communities and first-year residence halls (FYRH).

Logistic regression is used to estimate the impact of pre-entry and programmatic variables on retention while linear regression is used to estimate the impact of these variables on first-semester GPA. Because participation in the seminars, learning communities, and on-campus housing is dictated by the students' choice of major and the proximity of their home to campus, we contend sample selection bias is not an issue.

Because of the nonlinear nature of the logistic regression, the test statistic is a Wald chi-square, whereas the more familiar *t*-test is appropriate to linear regression.

Findings

First-year seminar participation alone has no statistically significant impact on the likelihood of retention, but it does have a statistically significant impact on first-semester grades (see Table 2). Even then, there is an important caveat to note. The numerical impact of the first-year seminar on grades (.144 GPA points) is almost entirely attributable to the fact that grades in these seminars are markedly higher than other 100-level courses that are not first-year seminars. This is not to say that the seminars have little purpose. These courses are typically (but not universally) part of learning communities, which had a modest effect on students' retention rates and a statistically significant impact on grades. Similarly, first-year residence hall participation had a modest effect on retention and a statistically significant impact on first-semester grades. In response to this and other data, ISU is moving to integrate first-year seminars, learning communities, and the residence hall experience into a living-learning community.

Table 1

First-Year Seminars at Indiana State University

Course	Title	Credit hours	Description	Population	Extended orientation	Intro to discipline	Study skills	Uniform across sections	Percent of sections in LCs
University 101	Learning in the University Community	2	A course to help students make a successful transition into the University by introducing the concepts and values of a university education, of liberal studies, and of preparation in the disciplines of study; by fostering a sense of tradition, community, and diversity of ideas and people; by developing critical-thinking skills as well as academic and personal skills necessary for success; and by providing an introduction to the resources and services of the University.	Athletes	Yes	No	Yes	Yes	0
				Academic Opportunity Program	Yes	No	Yes	Yes	33
				Open Preference	Yes	No	Yes	Yes	33
Nursing 104	Introduction to Nursing	2	An orientation course for students entering or exploring nursing as a possible professional career. Two classroom hours per week.	All nursing majors	No	Yes	Yes	Yes	80
Business 101	Freshman Business Experience I	1	A course designed to connect beginning students to college life and the College of Business. Students will learn behaviors and skills that will contribute to academic success and will learn about resources available in the academic community.	All business majors	Yes	Yes	Yes	Yes	100
MCT 131	Introduction to Manufacturing Technology	2	An orientation course for manufacturing technology students.	Manufacturing technology majors	No	Yes	Yes	Yes	100

Table continues on following page.

Table 1 continued.

Course	Title	Credit hours	Description	Population	Extended orientation	Intro to discipline	Study skills	Uniform across sections	Percent of sections in LCs
MCT 133	Introduction to Architectural and Construction Technology	2	An orientation course for architectural and construction technology students.	Construction technology majors	No	Yes	Yes	Yes	100
IMT 130	Introduction to Industrial and Mechanical Technology	2	An orientation course for students majoring in mechanical, automotive, or packaging technology.	Mechanical technology majors	No	Yes	Yes	Yes	100
AST 130	Introduction to Aerospace Technology	2	An orientation course designed for aerospace technology majors. Course includes University and department policies and procedures, aerospace courses, graduation requirements, and career aspiration and planning. Required of all students in the Department of Aerospace Technology.	Aerospace technology majors	No	Yes	Yes	Yes	100
ECT 130	Introduction to Electronics and Computer Technology	2	An orientation course for students majoring in electronics or computer technology. For beginning students.	Electronics and computer technology majors	No	Yes	Yes	Yes	100

Table 2

Impact of First-Year Programs on Student Retention and GPA

Programmatic variables	Logistic regression estimate on retention parameter	Linear regression estimate on grades parameter
FYRH	0.15	0.09**
FY Seminar	0.03	0.14**
Learning Community	0.18	0.09**

** $p < .01$

Contact

Robert Guell
Associate Professor of Economics and Coordinator of
First-Year Programs
Indiana State University
Holmstedt Hall 254
Phone: (812) 237-2169
Fax: (812) 237-7723
E-mail: ecguell@isugw.indstate.edu

Indiana University-Purdue University Indianapolis

The Institution

Indiana University-Purdue University Indianapolis (IUPUI) is a four-year, public institution with an enrollment of approximately 30,000 students, of whom about 22,000 are undergraduates. IUPUI was formed in the capital city from a consolidation of Indiana University and Purdue University programs in 1969 and is the third largest university in Indiana. The institution offers more than 185 academic programs from associate degrees to doctoral and professional degrees. Most IUPUI students commute to the campus, and the majority of entering students are first generation (defined as neither parent completing a four-year degree). The student body is mostly female (58%) with 14% of the population representing minority students, including 9.1% African American, 3.6% foreign, 2.7% Asian/Pacific Islander, 1.8% Hispanic, 0.3% American Indian/Alaskan Native, and 1.4% unknown.

The Seminar

First-year seminars, guided by a campus template that defines common learning outcomes and pedagogies, have been offered at IUPUI since 1997. Most undergraduate degree-granting units have developed their own one- to three-credit extended orientation versions of U110 and require them of their students. Exploratory students (i.e., those who have not declared a major) may take sections of the seminar offered by University College. An instructional team composed of a faculty member, academic advisor, librarian, and student mentor teaches each section.

Most seminars are linked to another first-year course, such as writing, mathematics, and other discipline introductions, to form a learning community. Since fall 2002, we have been developing themed learning communities (TLCs) that include a minimum of three first-year courses. In the TLCs, the first-year seminar functions as an anchor to integrate learning around a common theme among all the included courses. Approximately 100 sections of U110 (14 in TLCs) with a maximum enrollment of 25 students are

Institution Profile:

Indianapolis, IN

Public, Four-Year

29,860

Extended Orientation

Learning Community

offered each fall semester. Seventy-three percent of first-time, first-year students are currently enrolled.

Common learning outcomes for all IUPUI seminars include:

- Developing of a comprehensive perspective on higher education including a respect for diversity among individuals, communities, and disciplines
- Establishing a network of staff, faculty, and other students
- Understanding and practicing basic communication skills appropriate to the academic setting
- Beginning the process of understanding critical thinking
- Understanding and applying information technology in support of academic work
- Developing an understanding of one's abilities, skills, and life demands in order to pursue academic goals more effectively
- Understanding and making full use of IUPUI resources and services that support learning and campus connections

Research Design

Qualitative and quantitative approaches have been employed to comprehensively assess the impact of first-year seminar courses. These two approaches have been employed, not as two independent strands of inquiry and research, but as complementary techniques. In order to understand program-related effects, participants in first-year seminars are compared to non-participants with regard to academic performance (grade point averages) and one-year retention rates while controlling for student background characteristics and other academic support programs.

As we have improved our capacity to measure a wide array of student outcomes, it has become increasingly important that we develop ways to assess how our programs work to increase desirable outcomes and decrease undesirable ones. Qualitative evaluations provide the kind of in-depth process information that allow faculty, staff, and students to better understand when and how certain interventions are effective. Figure 1 displays our outcome assessment framework employing both qualitative and quantitative methods.

Findings

Results from a series of qualitative investigations (in-depth focus groups with student participants and responses to open-ended questionnaire items) have suggested that the most valuable aspects of the seminar experiences are the following: (a) having opportunities for interaction with other students, (b) having regular contact with advisors and faculty members, (c) learning to meet the demands of college (e.g., study skills, time-management skills, and expectations of higher education), and (d) gaining an understanding of available campus resources (e.g., Math Assistance Center, Writing Center, Career Center, and Student Activities).

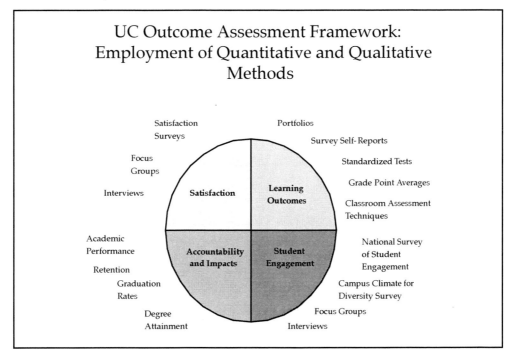

Figure 1. An Outcome Assessment Framework for First-Year Seminars Housed in University College.

Multivariate analysis of covariance procedures were employed to investigate impacts on grade point averages, and logistical regression procedures were employed to examine one-year retention rates. Table 1 shows the results of an analysis examining the impact of the first-year seminar courses on one-year retention rates. Although no significant differences in GPA existed between the two groups, participation in first-year seminars for fall 2001 had a rather dramatic effect on retention. Participation added an average of six percentage points to retention rates even after controlling for relevant student background and enrollment characteristics.

Shown in Table 2 are the results of analyses examining the impact of the seminar courses on one-year retention rates for fall 2002. Students participating in first-year seminars were retained at a significantly higher rate compared to non-participating students, even after controlling for student background and enrollment characteristics. There was a 9% difference in retention rates for participants compared to non-participants.

Results displayed in Table 3 suggest that conditionally admitted students participating in first-year seminars had significantly higher cumulative grade point averages compared to non-participating conditionally admitted students, even after controlling for student background enrollment characteristics.

Table 1

Impact of First-Year Seminars on One-Year Retention Rates for Fall 2001 Cohort (N = 2,410)

	n	Retention rate	Adjusted retention**
Non-participants	757	58%	59%
Seminar participants	1,653	65%	65%

Note. Adjusted retention controlled for differences in fall grade point average (not including seminar grade) and fall credit hours.
**$p < .01$

Table 2

Impact of First-Year Seminars on One-Year Retention Rates for Fall 2002 Cohort (N = 1,722)

	n	Retention rate	Adjusted retention**
Non-participants	493	58%	60%
Seminar participants	1,229	69%	69%
Overall	1,722	66%	

Note. Adjusted Retention controlled for differences in demographics, enrollment, academic preparation, and academic support program participation.
**$p < .01$

Table 3

Impact of First-Year Seminars on Academic Performance for Fall 2002 Regular and Conditional Admits

		n	Average fall GPA	Adjusted fall GPA
Regular admits	Non-participants	295	2.82	2.83
	Seminar participants	642	2.71	2.71
	Overall	937	2.75	
Conditional admits	Non-participants	186	2.13	2.07**
	Seminar participants	559	2.34	2.36**
	Overall	745	2.23	

Note. Average Fall GPA excludes seminar grade. Adjusted fall GPA controlled for differences in demographics, enrollment, academic preparation, and academic support program participation.
**$p < .01$

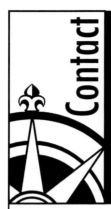

Contact

Barbara Jackson
Associate Dean of University College
815 W. Michigan Street, UC 3149
Indiana University-Purdue University Indianapolis
Indianapolis, IN 46202
Phone: (317) 274-8923
Fax: (317) 278-9656
E-mail: bjackson@iupui.edu

Additional Contributors:
Gayle Williams
Assistant Dean of University College

Michele Hansen
Director of Assessment

Indiana Wesleyan University

The Institution

Indiana Wesleyan University (IWU) is a comprehensive, private university with its main campus in Marion, Indiana. IWU's mission is to produce students prepared and committed to changing their world. An evangelical Christian commitment permeates the programming and culture and complements the campus focus on life purpose. Indiana Wesleyan enrolls more than 11,000 full-time students. The undergraduate population is 63.6% female and 81.3% White. Minority students include African Americans (2.3%), Hispanics (1.2%), Asian Americans (0.9%), and Native Americans (0.3%). The residential campus is considerably more homogeneous; 97% of its 2,600 students are White.

The Seminar

In 1999, the faculty unanimously voted to implement a three-credit liberal arts course that would meet key University mission objectives while also addressing student success principles. UNV180, *Becoming World Changers: Christianity and Contemporary Issues*, became the fulcrum of the entire curriculum for the residential campus. All new students on the residential campus (including transfer students) are required to take this course during their first year, and its credits apply toward general studies requirements.

Lecturers and facilitators for UNV180 are professors who have an established record of effective communication with new students. UNV180, an academic seminar with generally uniform content across sections, provides a common experience among all new students. Students learn the university mission and how it drives the various academic areas. This includes the integration of faith and learning. One of the key objectives is to help students understand their life purpose and how it relates to their college decisions. A complete description of course objectives is articulated in the syllabus and available on our web site at www.indwes.edu/unv180. This course has seven large (approximately 170 students) sections that meet twice a week and around 40 small (approximately 22 students) sections for breakout discussions on Fridays. Faculty or staff and peer leaders guide the smaller discussion sections.

Research Design

Since the introduction of the course in 1999, numerous instruments, both external and internal, have been used to assess student engagement and student satisfaction. The external tools were the National Survey of Student Engagement (NSSE), the College Student Experiences Questionnaire (CSEQ), the Student Satisfaction Inventory (SSI), and the Hope Scale, an eight-question survey that addresses student hope for fulfilling their dreams. Focus groups with students were also conducted. The Center for Life Calling and Leadership used an internal instrument (i.e., the Praxis) with all undeclared students.

Findings

NSSE data from 2004 reflect strong engagement among Life Calling students (the mandated "major" for undeclared students), particularly in the areas of classroom engagement. Students were also likely to work with classmates outside of class. Additionally, as would be expected with UNV180's emphasis on developing Christian values, our NSSE scores for participation in activities to enhance spirituality were high (see Table 1).

Table 1
2004 NSSE Results

	Indiana Wesleyan	Council of Independent Colleges	NSSE national norm
Asked questions in class or contributed	3.28	2.92	2.83
Made class presentations	3.08	2.48	2.23
Worked with classmates outside of class	3.08	2.45	2.39
Participated in activities to enhance spirituality	3.10	2.11	2.08

In 1996, the Student Satisfaction Inventory revealed that students considered advising important but were less satisfied than the national cohort (other private schools using the SSI) with their academic advising experience at IWU.

Three years after the implementation of the course, both the CSEQ and SSI reflected a positive change in student satisfaction with advising.

Before the implementation of UNV180, our SSI results also informed us of a pronounced need for more faculty contact and a common experience in the first year. Focus group follow-ups revealed the same. The course design addressed those needs by providing smaller discussion sections with faculty and requiring the seminar for all entering students. Within one year of implementing UNV180, SSI scores revealed dramatic improvement in both of these areas.

Conclusion

The implementation of this course has led directly to a $58,000 annual budget savings and indirectly to a $1.8 million dollar savings since its inception by contributing to the retention of students.

On the Marion campus, our retention rates grew from 68% to 81% from 1998 to 2002. Rates fluctuate around that mark each fall, despite rapid growth. The first-year course was implemented in the fall of 1999 and shows the strongest single correlation to this pronounced growth (i.e., 8% in one year). Four-year graduation rates jumped as well, increasing from 36% to 54% with the introduction of this first-year seminar. In this context, the sustained increases reflect remarkable gains.

Jerry Pattengale
Assistant Vice President for Academic Affairs
Indiana Wesleyan University
4201 South Washington Street
Marion, IN 46953
Phone: (765) 677-2170
Fax: (765) 677-2840
E-mail: jerry.pattengale@indwes.edu

Ithaca College

The Institution

Ithaca College, a selective four-year institution, enrolls approximately 5,700 undergraduate students on a residential campus in Ithaca, NY. Its School of Business educates approximately 550 undergraduates and 20 MBA students with a mission to help them "...develop managerial skills of a high order and acquire the requisite knowledge for making decisions that are both economically rational and ethically sound." The gender breakdown in the School of Business is approximately 60% male with about 11% of the students coming from typically underrepresented minorities including 5.0% African American, 5.0% Hispanic, and 0.5% Native American/Alaskan.

The Seminar

The College's first seminar approach on campus, *First-Year Seminar in Management*, was established in the School of Business in fall 1991. Its eventual replacement, *First-Year Seminar in Business*, has been required of all first-year students entering the Business School since 1998. Enrollment is limited to about 20 students per section and taught by tenured members of the faculty. Primarily an extended orientation seminar, the course demonstrates the relevance of many topics found in a typical "University 101" curriculum (e.g., diversity, time management) to students' ongoing individual career development in business settings.

Research Design

In fall 2000, 171 first-semester business majors co-registered in both *Introduction to Business* (Intro) and the *First-Year Seminar in Business*. Randomly, 77 students were placed in four seminar sections with curriculum linkages to *Introduction to Business*. The remaining 94 students were enrolled in one of five unlinked sections as a control group.

Three seminar themes—note taking, test taking, and writing—were coupled in the linked sections with the Intro curriculum. For example, the linked sections applied note-taking techniques to two lectures in *Introduction to Business*. Linked sections related test-taking skills material directly to the Intro course. Furthermore, the linked sections' term paper assignment focused on marketing, a topic that would soon be tested in their Intro course. These linkages were not offered in the control group sections. Statistically significant differences for outcomes between linked and unlinked seminar sections are reported below.

Findings

Introduction to Business examination grades correlated positively with registration in the linked first-year seminar sections. Registrants in linked seminars averaged 75% while their unlinked colleagues averaged 71%, a "C" versus a "C-" average grade respectively.

Students in the linked sections had an overall B grade point average; the unlinked registrants averaged B-. While just 55% of first-year business students were in unlinked seminars, 78% of all first-year business students on first-semester academic probation came from these unlinked sections.

While curriculum linkage did not improve overall retention to sophomore year, it correlated with retention in major to sophomore year—an important finding for campuses where FTE student statistics influence resource allocation among departments. Table 1 shows that 29% of the business students whose seminar was not linked to *Introduction to Business* did not return to the major in their sophomore year. Only 12% from the linked sections failed to return.

Table 1
Retention within Discipline by Seminar Curriculum Linkage (N = 171)

Sophomore Year Status	Linked (n = 77)	Non-Linked (n = 94)	Total
Returned to Business Major	68 88.3%	67 71.3%	135 78.9%
Left Business Major	9 11.7%	27 28.7%	36 21.1%

$p < .01$

In our study, 20 (56%) of the 36 students overall who did not re-enroll as business majors in their sophomore year dropped out; the remaining 16 (44%) had migrated to other majors on campus as their sophomore year began.

Contact

Donald Lifton
Associate Professor of Management
403 Smiddy Hall
Ithaca College
Ithaca, NY 14850
Phone: (607) 274-3234
Fax: (607) 274-1152
E-mail: Lifton@Ithaca.edu

Additional Contributors:
Alan Cohen
Associate Professor of Accounting

Warren Schlesinger
Associate Professor of Accounting

Kalamazoo College

The Institution

Kalamazoo College is a private, residential liberal arts institution located in Kalamazoo, Michigan, midway between Detroit and Chicago. The college enrolls 1,300 traditional full-time students who enter with an average ACT of 28 and average combined SAT of 1300. Women make up about 57% of the student body. About 80% of the students are White, 4.4% are Asian/Pacific Islander, 2.8% are African American, 1.4% are Hispanic, and less than 1% are American Indian. International students make up 2.1% of the student body; about 8% of students declined to indicate ethnicity. Typically, Kalamazoo College draws about 70% of its students from Michigan, with the remaining 30% coming from states across the country. Since the inception of a comprehensive study abroad program in 1962, 80% of our graduates have studied abroad for three to nine months. Kalamazoo students tend to be very academically focused, and many have an interest in the natural sciences. About 40% of the student body is engaged in community service during the academic year.

The Seminar

First-year seminars are the centerpiece of Kalamazoo College's First-Year Experience (FYE) program. Inaugurated in 1990, these academic seminars on various topics are vehicles through which students fulfill the writing requirement and serve as laboratories for considering important issues. Through special topics chosen by the faculty, the seminars introduce students to the critical thinking and writing skills required in college and include a particular emphasis on intercultural understanding in keeping with the international focus of the college. The approximately 20 seminars are small (15 to 16 students), begin during orientation, are required of every student, and operate primarily through a discussion rather than a lecture format. Though faculty from all divisions and most departments participate, the seminars are not introductions to the disciplines but rather explorations of an idea, topic, or event.

Institution Profile:
Kalamazoo, MI
Private, Four-Year
1,280
Academic w/Variable Content

Seminars are intended to help students find and develop a voice through writing, speaking, analytical reading, discussion, and critical thinking. They integrate collaborative and group work, peer review, and effective discussions, all of which promote student engagement. Students frequently write short papers, with many opportunities for revision. Each seminar participates in one class session called "Survivor in the Library: College Information Literacy Skills," intended to help students learn research techniques and apply them to a focused writing project. Three seminars are grouped into a thematic cluster called "Visions of America," which considers issues of race, gender and class through the lens of music, theater, and literature. Several seminars incorporate service-learning.

Students in each seminar have as their academic advisor either the instructor or one of several advisors linked to the seminar. Peer leaders assigned to each seminar serve as mentors to new students. A student tutor from the college's Academic Resource Center assists each seminar with writing projects.

Research Design

FYE is taking the lead in evaluative research at Kalamazoo College, both in assessing programs and reporting results, combining national surveys (including institution-specific questions) and home-grown instruments. All first-year students complete the in-house FYE@K survey early in the fall term. This survey focuses on orientation week, academic advising, the Summer Common Reading program, and peer leaders. Additional questions address the students' overall experience in the first few weeks at the college (e.g., making friends, managing time, being away from home, handling the coursework). Kalamazoo field tested The First-Year Initiative (FYI) Assessment in fall 2000, participated in a pilot administration in fall 2001, and has administered this survey to all first-year students at the end of fall terms in 2002, 2003, and 2004. Questions address quality of course instruction and academic/campus engagement.

Findings

Kalamazoo has taken a variety of approaches to assessing and improving our seminar program. Being able to benchmark our programs with peer institutions has been enormously helpful. In the FYI Surveys (2000-2004), Kalamazoo students have consistently ranked the seminars highly in areas such as usefulness of course readings, engaging pedagogy, improved critical thinking, improved connections with faculty, and overall course effectiveness. Kalamazoo's mean scores in these areas for 2003 compared to the weighted mean for all 51 participating institutions are shown in Table 1.

Table 1

Mean Scores for Selected Items on the First-Year Initiative (FYI) Assessment, 2003

	Kalamazoo	All institutions (N = 51)
Usefulness of course readings	5.81	4.36
Engaging pedagogy	5.59	4.69
Improved critical thinking	5.23	4.36
Improved connections with faculty	5.11	4.59
Overall course effectiveness	5.43	4.57

Note. Responses are on a seven-point Likert scale.

FYI results also demonstrated that students rated the seminars favorably in areas beyond stated course goals, such as time management (mean of 4.48) and out-of-class engagement (mean of 3.84). Both of these means were slightly above the means for all institutions. Results also clearly indicated that the seminars do not offer education about wellness, campus resources, and some other critical areas (means in these areas were below the all-institution means). However, the First-Year Forums, presentations designed to introduce new students to Kalamazoo College and the surrounding community, address many of these areas. Both the FYE@K survey and FYI Assessment indicated that students saw definite improvement in writing skills. While students gave high marks to class discussions, they felt less well trained to make formal class presentations. In the area of intercultural understanding, both instruments indicated that some seminars are doing better than others. Ultimately, shaping and modifying the first-year seminar is an ongoing process and is continually informed by the experiences of both students and seminar faculty.

Contact

Zaide Pixley
Assistant Provost for the First-Year Experience &
Director of Advising
Kalamazoo College
1200 Academy Street
Kalamazoo, MI 49006
Phone: (269) 337-5755
Fax: (269) 337-7182
E-mail: pixley@kzoo.edu

Additional Contributor:
Anne Dueweke
Assistant Provost for Institutional Research and Support

Kennesaw State University

The Institution

Kennesaw State University (KSU), located 20 miles north of Atlanta in Kennesaw, Georgia, is the third largest state university out of 34 institutions in the University System of Georgia. Founded in 1963, KSU is a comprehensive, public four-year institution offering more than 40 undergraduate degree programs. The growing student population exceeds 17,400 students (62% female and 38% male) and 63% of the first-year students are of traditional age (less than 20 years old). On-campus housing was introduced at this traditionally commuter campus in fall 2002, and KSU now provides accommodations (1,814 spaces) for slightly more than 10% of the student body. Ethnic students, of which 11% are African American, 3% Hispanic, 4% Asian/Pacific Islander, 2% multiracial, and less than 1% Native American, comprise 21% of the total enrollment. KSU's 1,472 international students (8%) represent 129 countries.

The Seminar

The first-year seminar (KSU 1101) has been taught since 1983 and is administered by the Office of Undergraduate and University Studies. The course is an elective, three-hour academic seminar with generally uniform core content delivered through common modules on transitional issues, academic skills reinforcement, values clarification, information literacy, ethics, diversity, leadership, and civic engagement. However, faculty may arrange their sections around a theme related to their personal interests. Maximum enrollment in a seminar is 25 students, and 45% of new first-year students enroll in the KSU 1101 course, which is taught by full-time faculty and staff members from across the campus. The course aims to:

- Provide students with practical skills and information for being successful in college
- Stimulate their thinking about the significance of a college education

Institution Profile:

Kennesaw, GA

Public, Four-Year

17,485

Hybrid

Learning Community

- Increase students' awareness of the self and the self in relation to others
- Foster tolerance for diversity
- Encourage students' planning for their academic and professional lives
- Promote students' community and civic engagement

The primary goal of the first-year seminar is to improve student persistence in college. Beginning students are introduced to academic life in an active, engaged small group environment. Surrounded by a small group of their peers, first-year students have the opportunity to learn about KSU and its resources, explore major and career options, and get to know members of KSU's faculty. Seminar instructors serve as academic advisors and mentors for students in their sections. More than two thirds of the 55 sections of KSU 1101 are linked in the themed **C**ommunities for **L**e**A**rning **S**ucces**S** (CLASS learning communities) program. The KSU 1101 course delivers integrated learning experiences for students in the two- or three-course cluster. Learning communities are required of all first-year residential students.

Research Design

The first-year seminar's impact on long-term student retention is probably the most difficult course objective to achieve and document. It may also be one of the most important for demonstrating the course's contributions to college student success. In an effort to explore the evidence of the relationship between first-time, first-year student enrollment in KSU 1101 and long-term student retention, one-year, two-year, and three-year retention rates were compared for students who took KSU 1101 with those who did not. First-year cohorts for fall 2000, fall 2001, and fall 2002 were initially examined separately to the extent that such long-term retention statistics were available. To increase the power of those statistical tests for the one-year and two-year retention rates, the fall cohorts were combined into single multiple-year samples, and retention differences were tested again. In order to explore the evidence as to whether the observed significant relationships between KSU 1101 enrollment and long-term retention applied to nontraditional age first-year students (age 20 or older) as well as traditional age first-year students (age 19 or younger), the combined samples were disaggregated by age group, and the retention distributions were tested using chi-square analysis. Even though it was not possible to control for all variables that might have affected long-term retention across the two comparison groups, the presence of statistically significant differences in the expected direction favoring KSU 1101 students was considered to be supportive evidence. Such evidence is consistent with the existence of a positive causal effect.

Findings

When each first-year cohort was examined separately, the differences in the one-year, two-year, and three-year retention rates appeared to be in the expected direction, favoring students who took KSU 1101 over those who did not. However, those percentage differences in retention were relatively small, and only half of them yielded statistically significant chi-squares at the .05 level of probability. The three tests that confirmed significantly higher retention for KSU 1101 participants included the one-year retention rates for the fall 2001 cohort (74% and 68%, respectively), the one-year retention rates for the fall 2002 cohort (78% and 73%, respectively), and the three-year retention rates for the fall 2000 cohort (51% and 45%, respectively). The other three tests for the one-year retention rates of the fall 2000 cohort and the two-year retention rates of the fall 2000 and 2001 cohorts yielded no significant differences, producing a mixed and inconsistent set of findings (see Tables 1 and 2).

Table 1
One-Year Retention Rates of KSU's First-Time, First-Year Students

Comparison groups		Beginning cohorts			Combined sample 2000-2002*
		Fall 2000	Fall 2001*	Fall 2002*	
Took KSU 1101	Percent retained	74	74	78	75
	N	638	681	803	2122
Did not take KSU 1101	Percent retained	70	68	73	71
	N	697	763	1163	2623

*p < .05

Table 2
Two-Year Retention Rates of KSU's First-Time, First-Year Students

Comparison groups		Beginning cohorts		Combined sample 2000-2001*
		Fall 2000	Fall 2001	
Took KSU 1101	Percent Retained	55	60	57
	N	638	681	1319
Did not take KSU 1101	Percent Retained	50	55	53
	N	697	763	1460

*p < .05

These mixed results were investigated further by increasing the power of the statistical tests through combining the fall cohorts into larger samples representing consecutive years. When those larger and more stable samples were tested, significant differences favoring KSU 1101 students were found for the one-year and two-year retention distributions (see Tables 1 and 2). Students who took KSU 1101 were four percentage points higher than those who did not take KSU 1101 in their one-year retention rate (75% and 71%, respectively) and in their two-year retention rate (57% and 53%, respectively). When the significant difference in the three-year retention rate for the Fall 2002 cohort was taken into account (51% and 45%, respectively), a consistent pattern of long-term higher retention favoring KSU 1101 students emerged for the three-year period under review.

Modest and significantly higher one-year, two-year, and three-year retention rates for KSU 1101 participants were found. Since this research design was not a controlled experiment, it is not reasonable to conclude definitively that the higher retention rates of KSU 1101 participants were caused by participation in that course. On the other hand, if such an effect did exist from the KSU 1101 or CLASS initiative, this data would be consistent with and confirm a modest positive relationship.

Hypothesizing that traditional-age students may be more likely to benefit from KSU 1101, we disaggregated the data by age and analyzed the retention rates of traditional and nontraditional students. Our analysis revealed that traditional-age students appear to benefit more from KSU 1101 than nontraditional-age students (See Table 3). The finding of no significant relationship between participation in KSU 1101 and long-term retention among nontraditional students is understandable. Older students tend to be more experienced in meeting life's challenges as well as more socially established than traditional first-year students. Older students may not need or benefit from the kinds of transitional support that are provided in KSU 1101 and CLASS learning communities. A different kind of first-year experience may need to be designed to aid retention of nontraditional students.

Table 3

Differences in the One-Year Retention Rates of KSU's Traditional-Age (<20) and Nontraditional-Age (>19) First-Time, First-Year Students

Comparison groups		Combined sample 2000-2002	
		Traditional age (< 20)*	Nontraditional age (> 19)
Took KSU 1101	Percent retained	77	58
	N	1,933	189
Did not take KSU 1101	Percent retained	73	61
	N	2,161	462

*$p < .05$

Two valuable tips for educational researchers also emerged here. One is that forming large samples of data from multiple years of experience may be key to generating the statistical power needed to document small but significant differences in the relationship between first-year seminars and student retention. The other is that the presence of nontraditional students in samples of first-year seminar participants may mask and/or depress retention statistics and comparisons for traditional students who are the course's primary target audience. Disaggregating the data by traditional- and nontraditional-age groups may be necessary to avoid this confounding effect when exploring the evidence of the effectiveness of first-year seminars.

Clearly, the evidence explored in this research on the positive relationship between the first-year seminar experience and long-term student retention produced encouraging results.

Contact

Ed Rugg, Director, Center for Institutional Effectiveness
Professor of Educational Research
Kennesaw State University
1000 Chastain Road #5400
IE/CETL House #54
Kennesaw, GA 30144-5591
Phone: (770) 499-3609
Fax: (770) 499-3253
E-mail: erugg@kennesaw.edu

Additional Contributors:
Donna R. Hutcheson
Assistant Director of Institutional Research

Kathy L. Matthews
Director, First-Year Experience, Department of University Studies

Medgar Evers College of The City University of New York

The Institution

Founded in 1970, Medgar Evers College of The City University of New York is a baccalaureate-general, public, urban, nonresidential college located in central Brooklyn, New York. The College offers both associate and baccalaureate degrees in liberal arts, sciences, and professional studies. The student enrollment is 5,000.

The majority of students are female (78%), low-income working adults (70%), and first-generation college students (85%). Their average age is 31 years. In fall 2003, 92% of the students were African American; 5% Hispanic; and 24% were immigrants from mainly Jamaica, Trinidad, Haiti, other Caribbean islands, and Latin America.

The Seminar

The Freshman Year Program (FYP) assists students with transitional challenges faced during the first college year by providing course instruction (Freshman Seminars), academic advising, and personal and career counseling. Freshman Seminars, *Introduction to College Survival Skills* (FS 101) and *Introduction to Critical Thinking Skills* (FS 102), are one-credit, first-year courses offered to Medgar Evers students since 1990 and required for graduation as a part of the College's core curriculum. Freshman Seminars provide an extended orientation to the rigors of college life and the culture of the institution and information on college survival, including study skills and are academic seminars on selected topics with generally uniform content across all sections.

These courses meet weekly throughout the 15-week semester. The average class size is 30 with a maximum enrollment of 35 students. FS 101 introduces incoming students to the challenges and requirements of college life. The course presents five interdisciplinary modules: (a) bonding, (b) orientation, (c) learning skills, (d) self-awareness, and (e) life success skills. This course also addresses student rights and responsibilities as they relate to the

Institution Profile:
Brooklyn, NY
Public, Four-Year
5,000
Hybrid
Learning Community

College, degree programs, and the structure and function of various offices. FS 102 reinforces the skills and concepts presented in FS 101 and focuses on career planning with an emphasis on gender-specific nontraditional careers.

Freshman Seminars are taught by full-time FYP instructors/counselors who must have at least a master's degree in counseling, psychology, or a related area. Freshman Seminar instructors/counselors also serve as academic advisors for each student in their classes. FYP counselors are responsible for assisting their students in developing an educational plan for the completion of their college degree. Early counseling intervention, referral services, and follow-up are also provided for crises and psychosocial challenges.

Research Design

The Collaborative Learning Community (CLC) is a FYP initiative instituted to improve academic performance and retention by fostering interpersonal relationships among students and promoting faculty and FYP instructors/counselors collaboration to provide students with cohesive interdisciplinary learning experiences and to monitor student progress.

In this program, two courses are "blocked" with a section of Freshman Seminar so that the same students take three courses together. Approximately 10% of the incoming first-year students self-select and enroll in the CLC.

Data from this program are analyzed to assess the effectiveness of the CLC in enhancing student retention and academic performance. The retention of first-year students in CLC and non-CLC classes was tracked beginning fall 2002. The two groups were the same demographically and in terms of remediation needs. Our research approach compared the two groups in terms of retention rates (by semester and at one year) and performance in selected courses.

Findings

Data indicate that the CLC enhances student performance and retention. Students in the CLC are retained at statistically significant higher numbers than non-CLC students (see Table 1). Retention for CLC students is 9% to 15% higher than for non-CLC students between fall 2002 and fall 2003.

Many Medgar Evers students (77%) require remedial coursework in order to meet the College's competency requirements in basic skills. CLC students complete this requirement in fewer semesters than non-CLC students. Seventy-five percent of CLC participants completed their remediation by spring 2004 compared with 68% of non-CLC students. This is important because institutional

Table 1
Persistence of First-Year Students in CLC and Non-CLC

	Population entering fall 2002	Retained fall 2003		Retained spring 2004	
		n	Percentage	n	Percentage
CLC students	180	170	94**	130	72**
Non-CLC students	2,617	2,213	85	1,489	57

Note. Non-CLC includes all incoming, continuing, transfer, and re-admitted first-year students enrolled during fall 2002, who attained 0 - 30 credits.

**$p < .01$

data indicate that student attrition positively correlates with the length of time taken to complete remediation.

Course instructors report no attendance problems and better overall academic performance ("C" grade or better) for CLC students compared with non-CLC students. For example, students in the CLC section of Introductory Psychology attained overall better grades in CLC courses than non-CLC sections of the same course. The comparison for fall 2002 indicated a 100% pass rate for the CLC section ("C" grade or better) compared with less than 50% pass rate for the non-CLC section. Approximately 50% of the CLC students achieved "A" grades.

Contact

Phyllis Curtis-Tweed
Associate Professor/Director, Freshman Year Program
1650 Bedford Avenue
Medgar Evers College
Brooklyn, NY 11225
Phone: (718) 270-4960,
Fax: (718) 270-5179
E-mail: ptweed@mec.cuny.edu

Additional Contributors:
Doris Withers
Professor/Vice President, Institutional Assessment, Planning & Accountability

Juollie Carroll
Professor/Director of Counseling Services

Gale Gibson-Ballah
Assistant Professor/Associate Dean, Student Advocacy & Support Services

Millersville University

The Institution

Millersville University, a regional, comprehensive, public university, is one of the 14 state-owned institutions of higher education that make up Pennsylvania's State System of Higher Education. Located in Millersville Borough, Lancaster County, Pennsylvania, the University enrolls approximately 6,800 undergraduate and 1,050 graduate students. More than 70% of undergraduates are full-time students. The student body is 60% female, 1 in 6 is at least 25 years of age, and 11% represent ethnic minority populations (African American 6.3%, Hispanic 2.7%, Asian American 1.7%, Multiracial 0.2%, and Native American 0.1%). More than 50% of undergraduate students live in either campus-owned or campus-related housing (privately-owned student housing immediately adjacent to campus).

The Seminar

University 101, "Freshman Seminar," is a one-semester hour, graded, elective course offered for entering exploratory (i.e., undecided) first-year students. The seminar is predominantly an extended orientation course with the inclusion of topical academic content related to the integrating theme course in a learning community. First offered in fall 2001, the seminar serves as the integral piece of a holistic living/learning community in which students are immersed. The living/learning community is a residential experience that includes special programming linked with the seminar and an array of related requirements (e.g., completion of a service-learning experience, attendance at co-curricular cultural and educational events, and participation in extracurricular activities) designed to foster student adjustment to college and full engagement with university life. Approximately 40% of eligible students choose to participate.

University 101 enrolls 23 to 25 students in each section, and University faculty members, who also serve as the students' advisors, teach the course. Peer mentors who reside with these

Institution Profile:

Millersville, PA

Public, Four-Year

7,861

Hybrid

Learning Community

students in the residence hall assist faculty in the seminar. A unique feature of Millersville's first-year seminar is the emphasis on problem-based learning to engage students in real-life situations they may experience on a college campus. Primary course goals include:

- Demonstrating strengthened inquiry, research, and information literacy skills
- Understanding and demonstrating tolerance for the relativity and plurality of human values and beliefs
- Recognizing personal strengths, limitations, and interests and formulating achievable educational goals
- Exploring various career opportunities
- Reflecting upon the importance of civic responsibility and academic integrity
- Understanding the importance of a liberal arts education

University 101 serves as the academic foundation for the exploratory living/learning community and is linked with two other courses: (a) either the required composition or communications course and (b) a content-based general education course that creates an integrating theme. Peer mentors play a pivotal role in facilitating transition by assisting with fulfillment of seminar objectives, providing additional programming within the residence halls on areas of academic and social success, and serving as mentors and role models for exploratory students. Attendance at extracurricular and co-curricular events and participation in an all-community service-learning experience are key components of the seminar requirements and are designed to facilitate community building and student engagement with the college experience.

Research Design

Quantitative studies compared second-year persistence rates and grade point averages between exploratory students who participated in the living/learning community and those who did not participate. For comparison purposes, SAT math, SAT verbal, and high school percentile rank scores as well as gender and race were used to determine if samples were equivalent. No significant differences in gender, SAT scores, or high school percentile rank were demonstrated between the study and comparison groups. The comparison groups had a higher percentage of ethnic minority students each year.

While it is not possible to distinguish between gains attributable to participation in University 101 as compared to participation in other courses within the living/learning community, non-participating students are taking essentially the same courses (i.e., composition, communications, and general education courses) without the integrating seminar and related experiences. They also do not have a common living experience.

Qualitative studies of students in the seminar included surveys that queried students on goal setting and attainment and most valuable seminar experiences. Seminar students also participated in focus groups.

Findings

Millersville researchers assessed initial effectiveness of the living/learning community with its University 101 integrating seminar in increasing second-year persistence and grade point averages for participating students. Results indicated that participating students were more likely to persist and earn acceptable grade point averages (a 2.0, C average, or above). The fall 2001 cohort demonstrated a second-year persistence rate of 85% as compared to a non-participant persistence rate of 78%, a non-significant finding. Significant differences were found ($\chi^2 = 11.12$, $p < .001$) in the analyses for the fall 2002 cohort, who demonstrated a significantly higher second-year persistence rate of 89% as compared to a non-participant persistence rate of 72%.

Researchers conducted t-test analyses to determine if first-semester grade point averages differed for participants and non-participants. No significant differences were found between these groups for the fall 2001, fall 2002, and fall 2003 cohorts.

Findings related to both second-year persistence rates and grade point averages of participating students are encouraging. However, this encouragement must be tempered with the knowledge that students self-select program participation, although the two groups do not differ with regard to entering academic indicators.

Qualitative findings indicated that goals of entering students concentrated around four themes: (a) being academically successful, (b) making friends, (c) getting involved, and (d) managing time effectively. When asked to identify the degree to which they succeeded in achieving these goals at the conclusion of the seminar, students ranked making friends and getting involved highest in goal attainment. Additionally, they set a spring semester goal of academic success in more than 70% of cases. Focus group findings indicated that students enjoyed being in a cohort, living together, and interacting with their peer mentor. The seminar experience was most valued for its relaxed atmosphere, lively discussions, problem-based learning experiences, and the dual teacher/advisor role of faculty.

Contact

Linda L. McDowell, Associate Professor
Coordinator, Freshman Year Experience
Millersville University
P.O. Box 1002
Millersville, PA 17551-0302
Phone: 717-871-2388 (phone)
Fax: 717-871-2251 (fax)
E-mail: Linda.mcdowell@millersville.edu

Additional Contributors:
Carol Y. Phillips
Executive Assistant to the President

Joseph Revelt
Director, Institutional Research

Moravian College

The Institution

Moravian College, the sixth oldest college in the country, is a four-year, private, undergraduate liberal arts institution in Bethlehem, Pennsylvania. It has a population of 1,452 undergraduates under the age of 25. Its students are predominantly White (non-Hispanic) (93.6%). The 6.4% of the population that are students of color are Hispanic (2.7%), African American (1.9%), and Asian American (1.4%). Moravian is primarily a residential college with two campuses approximately one mile apart. Approximately 70% of the students are residential, 8.4% live off-campus in nearby apartments, and 21.6% commute from home. The college gender ratio is approximately 60:40, females to males.

Institution Profile:

Bethlehem, PA

Private, Four-Year

1,850

Hybrid

The Seminar

The college has offered the first-year seminar, *Introduction to College Life* (ICL), for four years. It is a required graded course for all full-time, first-year students entering the college. The seminar is a hybrid combining an extended orientation and academic seminars on various topics. Students receive a half-course (i.e., two credits) unit of credit. Students also take a half course, *Concepts of Fitness and Wellness*, either in fall or spring semester. Together, both courses comprise The First-Year Experience. The maximum enrollment in each section is 19 students. The course is team taught by an instructor and an upperclass student advisor. The instructors are recruited from the college faculty and administration. They participate in a three-day training program as well as informal sessions throughout the fall semester. The Dean of Student Development chooses the student advisors, who also participate in multiple training sessions. ICL instructors serve as academic advisors to the students until the students declare a major, which cannot be done until after the completion of the first year. ICL advisors meet with their incoming students in May preceding their first year to help them plan their academic schedule. The advisors' second contact with students occurs during fall orientation. The ICL instructors meet with their incoming first-year students for a 90-minute discussion of a common summer reading, attend a public lecture by the author, and participate in a welcoming banquet. The ICL class meets once a week for 70 minutes for the 14-week fall semester. Following this, the meetings with first-year students become more informal, with the long-range goal of the program being to cultivate a mentoring relationship with the student even after the student declares a major. The whole course design, structure, and content is formulated to produce these student outcomes:

- A thorough introduction to campus and college life
- An understanding of student responsibilities as a member of the college community
- The development of a good relationship with an academic advisor
- An understanding of Moravian's Learning in Common curriculum and its relationship to a liberal arts education
- An individual plan for education at college and beyond
- Enhancement of both academic and personal coping skills

Research Design

The research strategy to assess the effectiveness of the ICL program consists of four components. One, all first-year students complete a standardized program assessment form. Two, the director of the ICL program conducts a focus group. Each ICL instructor is invited to nominate two students from her/his section to participate in this group. Three, upperclass advisors complete a standardized program assessment. Four, the ICL instructors also complete a standardized program assessment. All three standardized assessment forms have a set of eight questions that use a seven-point Likert-type scale (modified as appropriate, contingent on the audience) which are linked to the student outcomes. Each also has a series of open-ended questions asking the participants for feedback on the most positive and negative components of the program. The standardized questions have been the same for the past three years in order to benchmark improvements in the program.

Findings

The use of a standardized program assessment for students, peer advisors, and instructors allowed for multiple course comparisons on specific dimensions in a given year. Non-significant differences of one-way analyses of variance on these dimensions offered empirical justification for continuing the program in its present structure for next year.

A mastery approach to grading student performance in the course was adopted recently. This approach was introduced for a number of reasons. First, it empowered the first-year students by giving them control over the outcome of their grade in this course. As long as they completed all their work in a satisfactory fashion and on time, they knew that they would do well in the course. It also served as a diagnostic tool. If first-year students were falling behind in their assignments for this course, the instructor was quickly able to observe this and find out if this was also happening in other courses and discuss this with the advisee. It also helped to create a positive and supportive relationship between instructor and student. The instructor served more in a coaching role rather than as the evaluator of student performance per se. The descriptive statistics from students, upperclass advisors, and instructors were all favorable. The Likert-type scale went from 1 (strongly disagree) to 7 (strongly agree). In response to the statement, "the course grading procedures work well for this course," the student mean was 5.6 ($SD = 1.49$), the upperclass advisor mean was 6.05 ($SD = .97$), and the ICL instructor mean was 5.33 ($SD = 1.23$).

The most important investigation was the longitudinal analysis that compared the program on eight dimensions over three years (see Table 1). Thus, in each of the two most recent years, the program was benchmarked against the

Table 1
Longitudinal Analysis of ICL Program

Dimensions	2001-2002		2002-2003		2003-2004	
	M	SD	M	SD	M	SD
Positive advisor/ student relationship	5.14	1.64	5.20	1.49	5.31	1.58
Program goals & objectives clear	4.31*	1.81	5.02*	1.62	5.32*	1.55
Understanding of learning in common curriculum	4.43*	1.76	4.89*	1.63	5.29*	1.51
Assistance with course registration	5.57	1.64	5.63	1.59	5.75	1.61
Development of a personal education plan	3.64**	2.01	4.23**	1.96	4.47	1.91
Participation in community events	3.82*	1.98	4.22*	1.97	4.73*	1.79
Understanding of responsibilities as a member of a community	3.97*	1.75	4.38*	1.82	4.84*	1.68
Program helpful	3.80*	1.86	4.22*	1.92	4.63*	1.80

* $p < .01$ across all three years
** $p < .01$ between first two years

previous year's standardized program assessment results. On six of the eight dimensions assessed, the program has significantly improved over the past three years. The two scales that did not show significant improvement over three years (positive advisor/student relationship and assistance with course registration) were the two most highly rated dimensions at the start of the program, and the ratings continued to be strong. This quantitative analysis has been very helpful in justifying the continuation of the *Introduction to College Life* program, after it admittedly began with very modest results.

Arthur W. Lyons
Professor of Psychology &
Director of Introduction to College Life
Psychology Department
Moravian College
1200 Main Street
Bethlehem, PA 18018
Phone: (610) 861-1564
E-mail: lyonsa@moravian.edu

Mount Mary College

The Institution

Mount Mary College in Milwaukee, Wisconsin, is a four-year, private, Catholic, women's college with an enrollment of 1,600 undergraduate and graduate students. The majority of students are commuters (89.5%). Both traditional (68%) and nontraditional students (age 25 and older, 32%) attend Mount Mary College, and 26.9% identify themselves as minorities (16.4% African American, 4.4% Hispanic, 3% Asian/Pacific Islander, 0.6% Native American, and 2.5% unknown). The majority of Mount Mary students are the first in their families to attend college, with approximately one quarter of the students admitted in fall of 2003 reporting that a parent had earned a college degree.

Institution Profile:

Milwaukee, WI

Private, Four-Year

1,610

Academic w/Uniform
   Content

The Seminar

Mount Mary's first-year seminar, *Leadership for Social Justice*, is sponsored in part by the Fund for the Improvement of Postsecondary Education (FIPSE), U.S. Department of Education (2001-2004). This course, piloted during the 2001-2002 academic year, is an academic seminar with uniform content that introduces new students to the mission and vision of Mount Mary College. Although currently the three-credit course is not required, it is strongly recommended for all new, traditional-age first-year students. The average class size is 15 to 20 students. Faculty are seasoned instructors from a variety of academic disciplines (e.g., English, foreign language, business, anthropology, sociology, theology, and international studies) who teach the same content in each of their sections of the course and bring their own individual expertise to group planning and to teaching while sharing the common themes of the course. The primary objectives of *Leadership for Social Justice* are:

- To introduce students to Mount Mary's mission and the Mount Mary Women's Leadership Model
- To increase self-knowledge leading to an understanding of personal leadership styles

- To develop and increase skills and strategies for dealing with difficult issues and conflict
- To expand knowledge of local and global social justice issues
- To experience service-learning as a means of growing in leadership, self-understanding, and knowledge of social justice issues
- To develop reading, writing, and oral communication skills

Research Design

At the end of the semester, students completed a survey that asked them to assess their growth in attitudes and knowledge regarding race, class, and gender. Students also indicated how much their leadership abilities (e.g., collaborating with others and taking risks) had improved.

A second assessment tool required students' written responses to two scenarios and an advertisement (see Appendix). The scenarios presented situations that dealt with social justice issues in a systemic context. The advertisement was used to assess gender attitudes. This assessment was given at both the beginning and end of the semester, allowing for assessment of the amount of change in student responses.

Responses to the scenarios and advertisement were scored using a three-point rubric. Students were given points for the scenarios if they recognized multiple perspectives and social justice issues. For the advertisement, they were given points if they could articulate the implicit message (i.e., sex sells products).

Findings

Survey Data

A four-point Likert scale (1 = not at all, 4 = a great deal) was used to indicate growth in understanding and attitudes regarding gender, class, and race issues as a result of the leadership seminar. Growth in leadership abilities was also assessed. The means and standard deviations for responses are presented in Table 1.

Table 1

Mean Understanding, Attitude, and Ability Scores

Statement focus	N	M	SD
Understanding	1,094	3.46	.76
Attitude	1,095	3.18	.98
Leadership ability	840	3.48	.77

Note. Responses were made on a four-point scale (1 = not at all, 4 = a great deal).

These findings indicate that students who completed the leadership seminar believed that the course had a strong impact on their understanding and attitude toward systemic social justice issues and that their leadership abilities had improved as a result of the course.

Scenario Data

A total score was calculated for each student by adding the number of points she earned on the two scenarios and the advertisement. A related samples *t*-test was used to compare pre-course to post-course scores for each student. Results indicated that the post-course scores were significantly higher than the pre-course scores, $t(68) = 9.17$, $p < .05$, two-tailed, d = 1.10 (See Table 2).

Table 2
Pre- and Post-course Scenario Scores (N = 69)

Course	M	SD
Pre	3.63	1.27
Post	5.50	1.57

$p < .05$

Scenario Analysis by Individual Scenario

Individual analyses were conducted to determine if there was a significant difference between pre- and post-course scores for each scenario and the advertisement. Results of related samples *t*-tests indicated a significant difference in pre-course and post-test scores for each of the scenarios and the advertisement (see Table 3).

Table 3
Mean Scenario and Advertisement Scores Pre- and Post-Course

Source		M	SD
Scenario 1	Pre-course	1.30	.69
	Post-course	1.80	.70
Scenario 2	Pre-course	1.57	.76
	Post-course	2.22	.85
Advertisement	Pre-course	.78	.72
	Post-course	1.43	1.12

Note. Responses were scored on a three-point scale with a higher score indicating greater awareness and responsibility toward issues regarding race, class, and gender.
$p < .05$

In conclusion, students completing *Leadership for Social Justice* perceived growth in their attitudes, knowledge, and leadership skills as well as increased awareness and understanding of social justice issues in the areas of race, class, and gender. These findings suggest that a first-year seminar course that introduces students to issues of social justice and provides a firm academic foundation for discussing issues such as race, class, and gender has a positive impact on students' ability to critically assess and respond to these issues. In addition to having a positive impact on the students involved in the course, faculty development has also occurred as a result of the course, with more faculty focusing on social responsibility in their teaching. *The Leadership for Social Justice* course will have an impact on the curriculum in other disciplines as more departments add training in leadership skills, social justice issues, and service-learning to their courses.

Contact

Laurel End
Associate Professor
Mount Mary College
2900 N. Menomonee River Parkway
Milwaukee, WI 53222
Phone: (414) 258-4810, ext. 477
Fax: (414) 256-1224
E-mail: endl@mtmary.edu

Additional Contributors:
Phyllis Carey
Professor

Eileen Schwalbach
Vice President for Academic and Student Affairs

Appendix

Scenario 1

Jackie works at a manufacturing company in the heart of the city. Jackie can't afford a car, but she can easily get to work by taking a 10-minute bus ride. Last week, she learned that the company was moving to a suburb 20 miles from her home. In a letter to the employees, the management said they need more land to expand to remain financially viable. The new building would only be accessible by car since no bus lines go to that area. Jackie and nearly 300 other workers would not be able to get to their jobs at the new location.

Discuss the fairness of this situation.

Scenario 2

Julia is a player on the college soccer team. Last week, Martina, the coach, announced that the team will be able to order new uniforms this year and that a famous clothing maker is offering the college a significant discount if the college buys all of its uniforms from them. When Julia heard the name of the company, she hesitated and then said, "I'm wondering if we should place an order with that company. I just saw a television special, documenting that this company has factories in Indonesia and Honduras where the workers are paid less than $2 a day. The working conditions are unsafe."

"Really?" said Martina. "That's too bad, but I don't think we can let that affect our decision. We can't afford new uniforms without this discount. And besides, one team's decision won't change company practice anyway."

How should Julia respond to the situation?

Advertisement (description)

This advertisement was taken from a popular women's magazine. In the ad for leg glitter, two pairs of disembodied female legs are hanging out of a car window while an elderly woman is holding her hand over the eyes of her elderly husband.

Look at the ad. Ads contain many messages. What messages do you see in this ad?

Northern Illinois University

The Institution

Northern Illinois University (NIU) is a public, four-year institution located in DeKalb, Illinois. It has an undergraduate enrollment of approximately 18,250 and a total enrollment of approximately 25,250. It is primarily a residential campus for undergraduates, and 53% of undergraduate students are female. The fall 2004 undergraduate enrollment is composed of 83% traditional-age (18-22 years of age) students; and 25.1% are minority students, including 12.8% African American, 6.7% Hispanic, 5.8% Asian, and 0.2% American Indian/Alaskan Native. About 97% of new first-year students at NIU are in-state residents, and approximately half of each entering class are first-generation students. In this instance, first-generation students are defined as those students whose parents did not attend college.

The Seminar

UNIV 101: University Experience is an elective course taught during the first 12 weeks of the fall semester. Faculty and support staff with a master's degree and prior teaching experience are eligible to teach the course. The course was originally designed for students in health sciences majors and subsequently was expanded to be available to all first-year students. UNIV 101 carries one hour of academic credit and enrolls a maximum of 20 students in each section. This course is a basic skills seminar that is focused on the development of time management and study skills and improvement of students' academic and social adjustment to college. Extensive coordination across sections ensures generally uniform content. Approximately 43% of new first-year students are enrolled in UNIV 101, and student demand is consistently higher than the number of sections available.

The UNIV 101 course has three goals: (a) promote the establishment of relationships among peers and between students and the instructor; (b) provide enriching out-of-class activities and assignments; and (c) facilitate students' learning about the

Institution Profile:

DeKalb, IL

Public, Four-Year

25,260

Basic Study Skills

University and about their interests, abilities, and expectations in relation to their chosen field of study. To meet these goals, course context is designed to help students

- Understand the challenges and expectations of college
- Develop strategies for academic success
- Develop relationships
- Adjust to the university community and become involved
- Communicate with faculty
- Learn to manage time and money
- Learn how to use technology and NIU's resources
- Live in a diverse community
- Prepare for a career

Research Design

Research is conducted annually to assess the persistence and GPA of first-year students who enrolled in UNIV 101 and those who did not take the course. Longitudinal analyses are conducted to track student persistence each semester for their first two years at NIU. In addition, student GPA at the end of each semester is examined. In order to compare the performance of students who took the course and those who did not, statistical procedures (analysis of covariance) were used to control for any differences between the groups on ACT composite scores. At the completion of the course each fall, students complete a survey to assess their satisfaction with the course and the extent to which course objectives were accomplished. For this assessment, the persistence and GPA of 2,927 students who took the course between fall 1996 and fall 2001 were examined. Assessment findings from the student survey are based on the responses of 1,392 students who took the course during the fall 2003 semester.

Findings

Persistence

Assessment results indicated that 81.1% of the students who took UNIV 101 subsequently returned to the university for the fall semester of their second year, while 76.9% of the students who did not take the course returned for their second year of college. Consequently, the persistence rate of the students who took the course was significantly higher than for non-participants ($\chi^2 = 13.46$, $df = 1$, $p < .001$). See House, Xiao, and Rode (2004) for a more complete report of findings related to persistence.

Grade Performance

After controlling for differences between the two groups on ACT composite score, students who took the UNIV 101 course earned significantly higher mean first-semester GPAs (2.54) than students who did not take the course (2.42) [F (1, 13,366) = 6.55, p < .0001]. Assessment results indicated similar results for grade performance after two semesters. After accounting for ACT score differences, it was found that students who took the UNIV 101 course had a higher mean first-year GPA (2.62) than students who did not take the course (2.55) [F (1, 12,292) = 4.19, p < .0001]. See House et al. (2004) for a more complete report of findings related to academic performance.

Assessment Survey Findings

With regard to student perceptions of their academic success, 65% of the respondents indicated that the UNIV 101 course had contributed to their ability to succeed academically. Similarly, 74% of the students felt that the course had improved their awareness of their academic strengths and learning styles, 79% of the students indicated that the course improved their understanding of faculty expectations, and 89% felt that the course had increased their understanding of how to locate and use campus resources. Finally, 84% of the students felt the course had met or exceeded their expectations, and 79% indicated that they were satisfied or very satisfied with the UNIV 101 course.

Reference

House, J. D., Xiao, B., & Rode, D. (2004). *Academic outcomes of UNIV 101 new freshmen and other new freshmen (A follow-up assessment for fall 1996-fall 2001 cohorts)*. DeKalb, IL: Northern Illinois University, Office of Institutional Research.

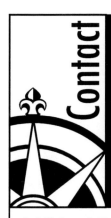

Contact

J. Daniel House
Director of Institutional Research
Lowden Hall 103
Northern Illinois University
DeKalb, IL 060115
Phone: 815-753-6002
Fax: 815-753-2566
E-mail: jhouse@niu.edu

Additional Contributors:
Denise Rode
Associate Director of Orientation

Beiling Xiao
Research Associate

Northern Kentucky University

The Institution

Northern Kentucky University (NKU), located in Highland Heights, Kentucky, is a public, urban, metropolitan university serving approximately 14,000 students in the Northern Kentucky and Cincinnati areas. NKU is primarily a commuter institution, though our residential population grew in 2003 to 1,000 students with the addition of a new residence hall. Approximately 10% of first-year students live on campus. According to the fall 2003 enrollment summary, the student population is 91% White, 4.8% African American, 2% international, and 2.2% other. Fifty-eight percent of students are female. Approximately 60% of the students at NKU are first-generation students: Neither their parents nor grandparents have earned a baccalaureate degree, though they may have had some college experience. As defined by the students' Pell Grant eligibility, 22% of them are classified as "low income."

The Seminar

NKU initiated a first-year seminar in 1986 using the University of South Carolina model, and we have kept that model since its inception. Our course, *Orientation to College and Beyond* (UNV 101), is a three-credit academic elective. The University 101 course is designed as an extended orientation seminar with a standard set of course objectives, though a few sections focus on more narrowly defined goals. Each fall, we enroll slightly more than half of the first-time, full-time students in UNV 101. With increasing enrollment over the past several years, we offered 60 sections for the fall 2004 semester. Faculty, administrators, and full-time professional staff at NKU teach the course, and they attend instructor training and ongoing workshops throughout the summer and fall.

We have designed the course with two guiding questions: (a) "*What* do students need to know and do in order to be successful in their first college year?" and (b) "*When* do they need to know and do

Institution Profile:

Highland Heights, KY

Public, Four-Year

13,945

Extended Orientation

it?" These two questions frame a set of 10 objectives that are common across all of our sections. These course objectives stress that students should learn about themselves as students and examine their values, create a community with other first-year students, learn to use NKU's resources and services, develop skills and knowledge to improve their academic success, learn more about diversity at NKU and in the world outside our campus, and learn to negotiate the "bureaucracy" of the university and its regulations, explore majors and careers, and more.

Our ongoing instructor workshops encourage engaging pedagogies that place students at the center of the learning experience. Students are seen as active partners in classes that often include group projects, hands-on activities, writing to learn, and participation in both academic and social co-curricular programs that encourage reflective learning (i.e., attending the extended question and answer session with the first-year book author or participating in the UNV 101 volleyball tournament followed by writing and discussion about what they learned from the activity). We attempt to help students understand more about themselves as learners by having them engage in activities rather than passively sitting in a classroom.

Because "one size does not fit all," we have developed a variety of sections that modify the focus of the curriculum to meet the needs of particular groups of students, such as undecided/undeclared students, or students in a particular major, residential students (a living/learning experience), African American students, Latino students, international students, or honors students.

Research Design

The Noel Levitz Student Satisfaction Inventory was administered as part of the Senior Assessment in November 2003. The Senior Assessment is a mandatory graduation requirement for students once they reach 90 hours of credit. Of the 400 students to whom the survey was administered, 180 included their social security number (which is optional), enabling us to analyze satisfaction data against specific variables. This analysis focuses on enrollment in a UNV 101 class as a variable.

In addition, institutional data from the 1996 and 1997 first-year cohorts (those most likely to be included in the Senior Assessment) were analyzed for graduation rates based upon enrollment in UNV 101 and subdivided by admission type.

For the cohorts in this study, there were three admission types: (a) regular, (b) stipulated, and (c) restricted. Admission type is largely determined based on a student's completion of the pre-college curriculum and ACT (or SAT equivalent) scores in English, reading, and mathematics. For instance, students who have an ACT score below 18 in mathematics are placed in a developmental mathematics course and can be considered stipulated because of that academic deficiency. Likewise, an ACT score below 18 in either English or reading will indicate a stipulated admission status for a student and will require developmental coursework in either writing or reading. Students will be admitted as "restricted" if they have not satisfactorily completed the pre-college curriculum and/or if they have a combination of two (or more) low ACT scores in mathematics, English, or reading. They are required to enroll in developmental courses to remediate the area in which they are academically deficient and are limited to enrolling in 13 credit hours per semester until they have satisfied the academic deficiency. The regularly admitted students have no academic deficiencies and are permitted to enroll in any college-level course (pending course prerequisites).

The importance of subdividing students by admission type becomes apparent when examining the data regarding graduation rates as admission type appears to be an important variable.

Findings

Former UNV 101 students are more satisfied. The Noel Levitz Student Satisfaction Inventory includes 82 items on which students rate their level of satisfaction (from 1 "not satisfied at all" to 7 "very satisfied") on a wide range of student issues.

Each of the five statements on which there was a statistically significant difference between UNV 101 and non-UNV 101 students' answers are discussed below along with the level of significance and an explanation of each finding.

1. "The campus staff is caring and helpful" ($p = .01$). The majority of our UNV 101 sections are taught by professional University staff members. In addition, UNV 101 students participate in activities and assignments that are designed to introduce them to University resources and personnel who can assist them with physical and emotional health issues, financial aid, career development, academic assistance, registration, or advising.

2. "Faculty care about me as an individual" ($p < .05$). In the UNV 101 class, students are required to write a faculty interview. The purpose of this assignment is to break down the barrier that often keeps a student from approaching a faculty member for assistance. They almost always leave the interview assignment with a sense that the faculty member is

a caring individual and this attitude may then transfer to their attitude toward other faculty members.

3. "Channels for expressing student complaints are readily available" ($p = .05$). Understanding the University catalog and college regulations and procedures is one of the objectives of UNV 101. For example, "Catalog Jeopardy," a popular activity that helps students learn about University procedures, is one of the more frequently used exercises on our Instructor Resources web page.

4. Though not to the same level of significance ($p < .10$), UNV 101 students responded more favorably to the approachability of administrators and the availability of financial aid. We believe both of these findings relate to course inclusion of activities related to campus procedures and the organization of the institution. The question of "how to get things done" on campus seems to be demystified after students have taken UNV 101.

5. A final question on which there was a slight significant difference ($p < .10$) is the response to "I can easily get involved in campus organizations." Close collaboration between the UNV 101 program and the Student Life office has led to classroom assignments that encourage students to seek out ways in which they can get involved in academic, social, or support organizations.

Former UNV 101 students have higher graduation rates. At NKU, there is a correlation between UNV 101 enrollment and a higher graduation rate. Analysis of the six- and seven-year graduation rates for students enrolled in UNV 101 as first-time, full-time first-year students at NKU demonstrates that those who enrolled in UNV 101, regardless of admission type, graduated at a higher rate. The case for supporting UNV 101's contribution to an increased graduation rate becomes more compelling when we disaggregate the students based upon their admission type. As explained earlier, the cohort in this study was enrolled under admission standards that specify three types of admission: regular, stipulated, and restricted. Whereas the overall difference between the six-year graduation rates for students who enrolled in UNV 101 versus those who did not was only 5%, the advantage changes dramatically when we look more closely at the students based on admission type (see Tables 1 and 2).

This advantage appears to be most acute when we look specifically at the students who are admitted as stipulated; there is a 12% to 13% difference in six-year graduation rate for the students who enrolled in UNV 101. These students' average composite ACT score is typically two points below that of the regularly admitted students, and yet there is only a 5% gap between the graduation

Table 1

Six-year Graduation Rates For Full-time, First-time First-Year Students Who Entered Fall 1997

Admission type	UNV 101		No UNV 101	
	Number	Percent graduated	Number	Percent graduated
Regular	307	42	333	39
Stipulated*	170	34	152	22
Restricted *	361	16	268	10
Overall*	838	30	753	25

*p < .05

Table 2

Seven-year Graduation Rates For Full-time, First-time First-Year Students Who Entered Fall 1996

Admission type	UNV 101		No UNV 101	
	Number	Percent graduated	Number	Percent graduated
Regular	189	47	262	43
Stipulated**	169	41	219	28
Restricted*	452	21	302	14
Overall	810	32	783	31

*p < .05
**p < .01

rate for the UNV 101 students in the stipulated category and that for the non-UNV 101 students in the regular admission category. There also appears to be a correlation between enrolling in UNV 101 and a higher graduation rate for students who are admitted as restricted. These students are our most "at risk" as they have the longest road to graduation (some are required to take nine, or even 12, credit hours of developmental course work), and they are the least academically prepared for the rigors of college work.

Conclusion

There seems ample evidence to conclude that the impact of UNV 101 resonates with our students beyond the first college year. This difference appears to be most significant when we look closely at the students who are coming into the institution with one academic deficiency. The difference diminishes when looking at the most prepared and the least prepared students. Perhaps it is the course's emphasis on becoming more knowledgeable about how the University works and getting connected to key administrators and staff as well as faculty that stays with our students throughout their years at NKU. We have designed the course with the desire to teach our students about the tools and knowledge they need to succeed. For the students entering their senior year satisfied with NKU, the seminar may have been one of the factors that enabled them to get to this point. Clearly we are not assigning a cause and effect relationship between UNV 101 and reaching senior class status, but a positive correlation does exist between student satisfaction and enrollment in UNV 101.

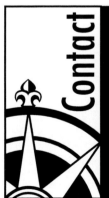

Vicki Stieha
Director of First-Year Programs
Northern Kentucky University
206 BEP
Highland Heights, KY 41099
Phone: (859) 572-5498
E-mail: stieha@nku.edu

Northern Michigan University

The Institution

Northern Michigan University (NMU) is a public, comprehensive, residential institution of 9,400 students located in Marquette, Michigan. Offering programs from diploma to master's degree, NMU provides access to students with widely varying academic abilities. Twenty percent of new first-year students are at risk (i.e., admitted on probation), and 32% are first generation (i.e., first in their family to attend college). Students are traditional in age (23), and more than half (54%) are female. The population is mostly White with 8% of the students representing minorities, including 2% Native American, 2% African American, 2% Multiracial, 1% Asian American, and 1% Hispanic.

The Seminar

NMU has offered UN100 (Freshman Seminar) since fall 1995. The two-credit, graded course is an elective for students admitted to the University in good standing and is required for students admitted on probation. A total of 48 sections are offered, 18 of which are for probationary students. Enrollment is limited to 25 students per section, and approximately half of our first-year students are currently enrolled in the course. University faculty and trained administrative staff teach the seminars. Primary goals are to help students develop strategies and attitudes to maximize academic success; to familiarize students with campus resources and how to use them; and to assist students in developing positive relationships with faculty, staff, student leaders, and peers.

NMU's seminars are blocked with three academic courses, meet for the entire semester, and vary to meet the programmatic needs of students. Primarily an extended orientation seminar, all sections address campus resources, learning strategies, student development issues, career counseling, academic advising, time and stress management, and study skills, among other issues. Sections for probationary students focus on basic study skills and advising (the instructor is also the students' advisor). Sections for undecided students emphasize career research and planning. Elective sections include discipline-linked sections designed to introduce students to the curriculum, faculty, and department relevant to their major.

As a result of continued growth (from 165 students in 1995 to more than 900 students in 2004) and the benefits realized by students (i.e., higher GPAs and better retention rates), we are in the process of developing a proposal to change our seminars from one semester to the full academic year.

Research Design

The underlying model guiding the First-Year Experience (FYE) research program at NMU is a Recurrent Institutional Cycle Design (Campbell & Stanley, 1963). This quasi-experimental design "...is appropriate to those situations in which a given aspect of an institutional process is, on some cyclical schedule, continually being presented to a new group of respondents" (p. 57).

Beginning with the first-year seminar in fall 1995 and continuing through fall 2004, intact cohort groups of UN100 and Non-UN100, first-time, full-time new students have been tracked and their academic progress has been monitored each semester for up to seven years. Grade point averages and retention and graduation rates are routinely collected and widely shared with FYE leadership and academic administration. Extensive focus group activity and end-of-course assessments continue to evaluate, shape, and improve the FYE program.

Findings

Underlying this academic and student support model is an extensive program of quantitative research that has consistently illustrated that UN100 participation is related to higher than expected rates of retention and graduation and improved academic performance. Second- and third-year retention rates, as well as graduation statistics, are based on the experiences of thousands of NMU students. Table 1 presents the results from multiple new student cohorts.

While the retention findings could have been anticipated based on the extant literature, an unexpected but positive impact has been shown with regard to first-semester grade point averages. As seen in Table 2, students who participate in the first-year seminar demonstrate an advantage in first semester performance in comparison to non-UN100 first-year students whose credentials are comparable or slightly higher at the beginning of college.

Table 1

Comparative Retention and Graduation Rates for UN100 Versus Non-UN100 First-Year Students, Fall 1995 – Fall 2002

Percent persisting to:	UN100 first-year students ($N = 3,133$)	Non-UN100 first-year students ($N = 7,537$)
Second year*	72.0	67.5
Third year	60.6	53.9
Fourth year	54.8	47.8
Percent graduating	47.0	44.6

Note. Graduation rates based on minimum of five years.

*$p < .05$

Table 2

Comparative First-Semester College GPA for UN100 Versus Non-UN100 First-Year Students, Fall 1995 – Fall 2003

	UN100 first-year students ($N = 3,835$)	Non-UN100 first-year students ($N = 8,365$)
Fall 1995	2.42	2.46
Fall 1996	2.52	2.25
Fall 1997	2.71	2.31
Fall 1998	2.46	2.35
Fall 1999	2.62	2.44
Fall 2000	2.39	2.43
Fall 2001	2.62	2.58
Fall 2002	2.66	2.50
Fall 2003	2.59	2.53
Overall*	2.58	2.43

Note. Overall GPA was weighted by semester enrollments.

*$p < .05$

Another positive finding involves the percentage of new first-year students who attain at least a "C" (2.00 GPA) average in their first semester at NMU. The importance of the first academic semester on retention and long-term college success is well documented. The finding that a higher percentage of UN100 students attain this level of satisfactory academic progress is shown in Table 3.

Table 3

Comparative First-Semester Clear Standing for UN100 Versus Non-UN100 First-Year Students, Fall 1995 - Fall 2003

	UN100 first-year students (N = 3,835)	Non-UN100 first-year students (N = 8,365)
Fall 1995	70.3%	67.2%
Fall 1996	77.6%	65.5%
Fall 1997	82.8%	67.6%
Fall 1998	72.9%	70.0%
Fall 1999	79.1%	73.1%
Fall 2000	71.7%	72.3%
Fall 2001	79.2%	77.0%
Fall 2002	80.1%	74.4%
Fall 2003	78.6%	74.9%
Overall*	77.7%	71.2%

Note. Clear standing is defined as a first-semester GPA of 2.00 or higher. Overall percent is weighted by semester enrollments.
*$p < .05$

In terms of qualitative findings, individual seminar courses, instructors, and teaching assistants are evaluated by students participating in the program. Results indicated that 92% to 95% of students agreed or strongly agreed that the program met or exceeded their expectations and that course instructors and teaching assistants were effective and supportive. Most notable was the students' feeling of comfort with the University and the fact that they would recommend the course to incoming students.

Reference

Campbell, D. T., & Stanley, J. C. (1963). *Experimental and quasi-experimental designs for research.* Chicago: Rand McNally College Publishing.

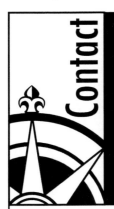

Contact

Susan VerDuin
Coordinator, First Year Programs
Northern Michigan University
1401 Presque Isle Avenue
Marquette, Michigan 49855
Phone: (906) 227-1459
Fax: (906) 227-1714
E-mail: sverduin@nmu.edu

Additional Contributor:
Paul Duby
Associate Vice President for Institutional Research

Occidental College

The Institution

Occidental College is a four-year, private, residential liberal arts college located in Los Angeles, California. The College has a total enrollment of 1,800 students, 98% of whom are between 17 and 22 years of age. All first-year students are required to live on campus; about 20% of non-first-year students live in off-campus housing near the college. The student body reflects the racial and ethnic diversity of southern California: 55.9% White, 14.2% Latino, 14% Asian, 6.9% African American, 3.5% international, and 1.3% Native American. Women comprise 56.4% of the student body. Approximately 16% of our students are the first members of their family to attend college.

Institution Profile:

Los Angeles, CA

Private, Four-Year

1,858

Hybrid

Learning Community

The Seminar

Every first-year student is required to take a skills-intensive, content-based "Core Seminar" during his/her first semester at Occidental. Rather than offering multiple sections of the same seminar to all students, we have decided to offer a wide range of academic seminars on different topics that incorporate elements of an extended orientation course. In fall 2004, the entering class will select from among 32 seminars, including:

- CSP 1: Investigating the Global Economy (Economics)
- CSP 4: Voices of Protest: The 1960s in History and Memory (History)
- CSP 7: Meaning and Purpose in the Gardens of China and Japan (Art History and the Visual Arts)
- CSP 10: Feminism and Philosophy (Philosophy)
- CSP 14: Crisis in American Education (Education)
- CSP 17: Microbes Got Game: Epidemics and Pandemics (Chemistry)
- CSP 19: The Unbearable Whiteness of Barbie: Race and Popular Culture in the United States (Anthropology)
- CSP 28: Masterpieces of Russian Fiction: Classic Literature, New Perspectives (German, Russian, and Classical Studies)

- CSP 31: What It Means to Be a Person (Philosophy)
- CSP 32: Poets, Painters and Politics: Latin American Icons and Vocational Calling (Spanish)

Students receive four units of credit (same as for "regular courses") for these seminars, nearly all of which are taught by tenure-track members of the faculty. Enrollment is limited to 16 students per section. The goals of the Core Seminars include: (a) enhanced critical thinking, analytical reading, and expository writing; (b) deeper engagement with the college community; and (c) improved retention. We have offered various versions of a Core Seminar to entering students for more than 16 years (i.e., linked to another course, "stand alone," or linked to residence halls), and we have discovered that the effectiveness of the seminar changes when we *change the way we offer it*. Based on the positive results of a yearlong pilot program (2001-2002) that compared the effectiveness of "stand-alone seminars" with seminars linked to residence halls, we now place all students in every Core Seminar together in the same residence hall, forming what we call Living and Learning Communities (LLCs). Our ongoing assessment of this implementation of the Core Seminars leads us to conclude that the LLC format has contributed, at least in part, to the students' increased sense of community and to improved retention rates.

Research Design

Efforts were undertaken to assess the effectiveness of the LLC program both during its pilot phase (academic year 2001-2002) and during its full phase, when the program was introduced to the entire entering class (academic year 2002-2003). Data were collected in the fall and spring of both academic years. At all four time-points, students responded to a survey regarding their experiences in their Core Seminar and their feelings of connection to the Occidental community on a seven-point Likert scale ranging from 1 (*Never*) to 7 (*Frequently*). Students were also asked to provide written comments about their experiences in their Core Seminar. The survey instrument was modified slightly in Year 2 of the study.

In the spring of the full phase of the project, sociometric data were collected from participating students. Students were given an alphabetized list of all of the first-year students and were asked to circle the names of all the students with whom they studied on a regular basis. Students were identified as study partners if they reciprocally nominated each other.

Three hundred and eighty-seven (53 LLC and 325 non-LLC) first-year students (82.53% of the first-year class) participated in the pilot assessment. In the full phase of the project, 336 first-year students (76.19% of the entering class) completed the survey instrument. Of those students, 263 (59.63% of the entering class) also completed the sociometric measure.

Findings

A series of univariate analyses of variance were conducted in order to compare the fall survey responses of the participants. As shown in Table 1, the results indicate that LLC students differed significantly from a matched sample of non-LLC students in their responses to 6 of 17 survey items (the students were matched on gender, race/ethnicity, and verbal SAT score). Three items indicated that students in the LLC reported seeking more academic support from their classmates than non-LLC students (e.g., "I showed drafts of my papers to other students in my Core class."). Three additional items suggest that students in the LLC felt a stronger sense of community than non-LLC students (e.g., "My Core class provided me with a sense of community."). The results were generally consistent from fall to spring.

Table 1
Means and Standard Deviations on Survey Items Indicating Significant Differences Between LLC and Non-LLC Students

Survey item	Matched participants			
	LLC students		Non-LLC students	
	M	*SD*	*M*	*SD*
Academic support				
Worked with peers on assignments	5.24*	1.72	4.24*	2.13
Showed drafts of papers to peers	4.97*	1.84	3.67**	1.92
Count on peers for academic support	5.46***	1.46	4.05***	1.72
Connection to community				
Class provided community	5.46**	1.36	4.37**	1.72
Closest friends in class	4.74***	1.31	3.39***	1.67
Socialize with peers from class	5.31***	1.37	3.78***	1.86

*p < .05
** p < .01
*** p < .001

The results also showed that there was an interaction between fall GPA and students' sense of belonging to the Occidental community in the prediction of students' spring GPA, $F (3, 246) = 7.68$, $p < .01$. The grades of students who indicated that they did not feel connected to the Occidental community in the fall dropped significantly from fall to spring. In contrast, the grades of students who indicated that they either felt moderately or highly connected to the Occidental community in the fall did not change significantly from fall to spring.

These findings point to the relationship between students' sense of connectedness to the institution in their first semester and their academic performance. Thus, LLCs indirectly help students' grades.

The self-report data collected during the full phase of the program again indicated that students felt connected to the Occidental community and sought out academic support from their peers. The data obtained using the sociometric nomination measure validated this self-report data. The results indicated that the number of study partners that students had ranged from 0 to 12 (the mean number of reciprocal study partners was 2.20 with a standard deviation of 2.17). The majority of students (74.90%) had one or more reciprocal study partners. Students' endorsement of the peer support items on the supplemental survey correlated positively with their number of reciprocal study partners.

Conclusion

Our first-year seminars seem to work most effectively in the LLC format. Students in LLC seminars report that they discuss their reading and writing assignments with each other more frequently than students in stand-alone seminars, in part, because they are grouped in residence halls with other students who share at least one of their classes. In addition, students in LLC seminars feel a stronger connection to Occidental College than students in stand-alone seminars. Happily, this format also meets the desires and needs of the faculty and the institution better than other formats we have used in the past. Faculty members report that they enjoy teaching small seminars in their areas of expertise rather than having to "work up" a course on a common topic taught by all seminar instructors. In addition, from an institutional perspective, it is clearly easier to sustain the quality of the program as a whole when faculty members are eager to teach in it.

Contacts

Andrea Hopmeyer-Gorman, Associate Professor of Psychology
Occidental College, Department of Psychology
Los Angeles, CA 90041
Phone: (323) 259-2788
E-mail: ahgorman@oxy.edu

Eric Newhall (main contact for Center), Associate Dean of
the College, Core Program Director, Professor of English and
Comparative Literary Studies, Occidental College
Core Program Office
Los Angeles, CA 90041
Phone: (323) 259-2859
Fax: (323) 341-4942
E-mail: newhall@oxy.edu

Additional Contributor:
Jonathan Nakamoto
Graduate Student, Department of Psychology
University of Southern California

Olympic College

The Institution

Olympic College, located in Bremerton, Washington, enrolls 4,644 full-time equivalent (FTE) students with a headcount of 11,637. As a public, two-year institution, Olympic College is a commuter campus. The median age is 25.5. Fifty-seven percent of the student body is female. Students identify themselves as part of the following racial groups: 74% White, 9% Asian/Pacific Islander, 3% African American, 3% Hispanic, and 2% Native American. Eight percent of the students identify themselves as "other" or did not identify with a particular group.

The Seminar

Strategies for Academic Success (General Studies 100) is a combination extended orientation and study skills course, which has been offered for five years. It is required for students who place into developmental English courses and is linked with those courses. It is an elective for all other students. This is a two-credit course and the maximum enrollment for each section is 25. The course is offered in a variety of modalities, including an online section, an intensive pre-fall quarter section, linked developmental English sections, and stand-alone sections. Approximately 35% of first-year students are enrolled in the course. Adjunct faculty and tenured faculty from counseling, the library, education, business, and English deliver instruction for the class.

The learning outcomes for the course are as follows:

- To demonstrate knowledge of the purposes, values, and expectations of higher education
- To demonstrate basic self-awareness and self-management
- To demonstrate academic skills of learning how to learn
- To write an educational/career plan
- To demonstrate knowledge of physical, social, and emotional wellness

Institution Profile:

Bremerton, WA

Public, Two-Year

7,102

Hybrid

Learning Community

Research Design

The EBI First-Year Initiative Survey was administered for the first time in 2003-04. A comparison of Olympic College results with Carnegie Class institutions was provided. In addition, students were given an opportunity to provide qualitative input at the end of the quarter by addressing (a) what worked well in the class, (b) how the student will use strategies learned in class, and (c) suggestions for course improvements. Lastly, student retention data were gathered on the students enrolled in the course.

Findings

The survey response rate among fall quarter 2003 students enrolled in General Studies 100 is 40% ($N = 115$). Responses were gathered from students enrolled in linked, online, intensive, and stand-alone courses. When comparing Olympic's top predictors of overall course effectiveness to other institutions within its Carnegie Class, Olympic outperformed on most measures including usefulness of course readings, pedagogy engagement, and overall course effectiveness (see Table 1).

Table 1
Comparison of Olympic College Top Predictors of Overall Course Effectiveness With Carnegie Class Institutions

	Olympic College mean	Carnegie mean
Top Predictor: Usefulness of Course Readings	**5.16**	**4.44**
Course readings were helpful	5.33	4.54
Course readings were relevant	5.18	4.55
Course readings were interesting	4.97	4.21
Second Predictor: Course Included Engaging Pedagogy	**5.07**	**4.72**
Encouragement for students to work together	5.49	5.07
Encouragement to speak in class	5.22	4.99
Meaningful class discussions	5.15	4.84
A variety of teaching methods	5.07	4.84
Productive use of class time	4.98	4.79
Meaningful homework	4.86	4.40
Challenging assignments	4.72	4.12
Overall Course Effectiveness	**5.02**	**4.51**
Student would recommend this course to other first-year students	5.34	4.51
Contributed to the ability to succeed academically	5.10	4.57
Contributed to the ability to adjust to the college social environment	4.91	4.61
Covered topics important to student	4.89	4.35
Included interesting subject matter	4.85	4.44

Table 2 illustrates the questions on which Olympic College scored the highest and lowest on nationally normed questions included on the First-Year Initiative (FYI) Assessment.

Table 2

Highest and Lowest Means on Nationally Normed Questions

Item	Mean
Highest means	
Would recommend this college to a friend	5.96
Want to return to this college for the next term	5.86
Had a high-quality learning experience	5.65
Improved their understanding of the impact of establishing personal goals	5.56
Were encouraged to work together	5.49
Improved completing homework assignments on time	5.36
Increased their understanding of library resources	5.34
Found course readings helpful	5.33
Improved their understanding of academic strengths	5.30
Lowest means	
Increased participation in campus-sponsored organizations	2.81
Increased their attendance at campus cultural events	2.81
Improved their understanding of wellness issues such as the impact of drug and alcohol consumption and the impact of exercising regularly	3.73
Improved their oral presentation skills	4.05

Note. Rating scale of 1 (not at all) to 7 (significantly)

In addition to data gathered via the survey, institutional measures indicate that the fall 2003 to winter 2004 retention rate improved upon its historical first to second quarter average from 51% to 68%. Many students attending community colleges possess at least one, or perhaps several, risk factors for leaving higher education, which include entering at a pre-college skill level, being a first-generation college student, attending part-time, and being a single parent. Two thirds of the students who participated in this study were in developmental

English classes, an indication they had at least one risk factor. The combination of both Olympic College retention data and the assessment information provided through the EBI First-Year Initiative (FYI) Assessment indicates that the General Studies course is having a positive impact on student success.

Additionally, analysis of student written feedback revealed specific themes regarding what worked well in the class, how the students intended to apply strategies learned in class, and what needed improvement.

In their assessment of the General Studies 100 classes, students highlighted those activities that they thought worked especially well for them. These activities included assessment and understanding of learning styles, group discussions, guest lectures, knowledge about note and test taking, and development of critical-thinking skills. Students indicated that they intended to use strategies that they learned in class, including note taking, memory, and study skills; time management; respect for and awareness of diversity and cultural issues; and education and career planning. Suggestions for improvement included more hands-on, in-class activities; requests for offering the class with more credit and class time assigned to it; and continued inclusion of guest speakers.

Conclusion

Potential future research and assessment could include a focus on each course modality to determine whether or not there are significant differences in results with regard to online sections, linked sections, intensive pre-fall sessions, and stand-alone sections. The results of the initial EBI First-Year Initiative (FYI) Assessment will be used to guide future curriculum revision and development. Specific changes for 2004-05 include addressing ways to encourage more student involvement in campus and cultural activities, exploring the option of linking the course with a health and wellness course offered through the physical education department, promoting active learning, and providing opportunities to develop oral presentation skills.

Contact

Gina Huston
Dean of Student Development
Olympic College
1600 Chester Avenue
Bremerton, WA 98337-1699
Phone: (360) 475-7535
Fax: (360) 475-7233
E-mail: ghuston@oc.ctc.edu

Rocky Mountain College

The Institution

Founded in 1878, the oldest institution of higher learning in the state of Montana, Rocky Mountain College (RMC) is a private, residential, liberal arts college located in Billings. In 2003, 65% of RMC's 935 students (928 FTE) came from within the state and generally reflected the region's rural demographics. Over the last three years, 53% of the undergraduate student body has been female. RMC's unique student population also includes 41% first-generation college students who report that neither their mothers nor fathers graduated from college. In addition, RMC's student population has 13% ethnic minorities (compared to 8% state-wide), with 8% of that population being American Indian, 2.5% Hispanic, 1% African American, and 1% Asian or Pacific Islander. Six percent of the student body comes from foreign countries. While the College is relatively small in the sphere of regional higher education, its size still presents a challenge to many of its students, as more than 50% of RMC students graduated from a high school with fewer than 100 classmates, and nearly 30% had fewer than 50 classmates.

The Seminar

The concept of the Rocky Freshman Experience (RFE) grew from research compiled in the mid-1990s by Ron Cochran and Jay Cassel, two RMC faculty members. They concluded that Rocky Mountain students who associated with small groups connected to areas of interest, such as the football team or choir, were retained at higher rates than those who did not. These findings suggested that requiring students to be involved in selective learning communities would benefit the College's retention efforts. In the four years since RFE was established, it has been required of all new first-year students. Incoming students choose from a variety of "content" (discipline-specific) classes consisting of two to four credits linked to English 119, the first-year writing course for three credits, and Rocky 101, the "introduction to college" course (one credit) for a total program of six to eight credits. All sections

Institution Profile:
Billings, MT
Private, Four-Year
938
Extended Orientation
Learning Community

are limited to 22 students. "Content" courses from which students may choose have varied over the years and have included biology, sociology, drawing, art history, music, cinema, history, environmental studies, ecology, business, humanities, and philosophy.

The College pays regular, full-time faculty to create these coupled classes and attend each other's classes as "students." A variety of staff members, counselors, and other student service personnel teach Rocky 101, providing students a healthy exposure to first-year success strategies and the uniqueness of the RMC experience. An extended orientation course, Rocky 101 meets twice a week for half of the semester. Instructors stress college survival skills and help students work with their advisors in planning their academic careers. The class also serves as a safe place for students to voice their concerns in natural social groups.

Research Design

A variety of research methods are employed by the college to test the effectiveness of the RFE program. To provide baseline data, incoming students are given a pre-enrollment student survey (i.e., College Student Expectations Questionnaire) as well as a questionnaire containing additional questions. Four weeks into the semester, the dean of students asks faculty to provide the names of all students who are experiencing difficulty making the transition to college life manifested through attendance issues or poor academic progress. Depending on the problem identified by the faculty, a variety of responses may be put in place by administration, student services personnel, or academic staff. The associate academic dean administers end-of-semester and end-of-year surveys concerning student progress and satisfaction. Also, at the end of the year, the English faculty monitor student progress by gathering portfolios of student writing assignments, which are in turn analyzed by an external reviewer.

Findings

The English program's goals for its portion of the RFE focus on the student's ability to write an effective thesis statement; write a convincing argument with acceptable grammar, punctuation, and mechanics; and develop skills in critical reading. By 2004, 86% of first-time, first-year students thought their ability to develop a thesis statement was better than before the start of college writing; 90% believed they could write a more convincing argument; 81% saw their ability to write with acceptable grammar, punctuation, and mechanics as better than when they began; and 83% felt they had strengthened their critical reading. The English faculty's examination of student writing portfolios confirms students' perceptions of their own progress.

Another important RFE goal is to increase student participation in the campus-wide academic advising and academic tutoring programs. By 2004, 98% of first-year students were able to identify their academic advisor by the end of the academic year, and 85% of first-year students stated that their academic advisor was effective in helping them meet their academic goals. Although 90% of entering students stated they were well aware of the College's academic tutoring programs, only 34% participated in the programs over the course of the year. The retention of first-year students has increased 7% since the institution of RFE. The remainder of the data indicates that the students feel the writing portion of RFE is well coordinated with the content course and that they have an idea of how disciplines interrelate. A majority of students feel the seminar generates good discussion about college life, is relevant to the initial adjustment stage, and helps them reorganize and address the major challenges associated with the first-year experience.

Contact

David Reynolds
Associate Dean for Advising and Assessment
Rocky Mountain College
1511 Poly Drive
Billings, MT 59102
Phone: (406) 657-1112
E-mail: reynoldd@rocky.edu

Additional Contributors:
Jacqueline Dundas
Director of the Rocky Freshman Experience, Instructor of English

Brad Nason
Dean of Students

Rollins College

The Institution

Rollins College is a private, four-year, comprehensive liberal arts institution located in Winter Park, Florida. Rollins enrolls 1,733 undergraduate day students. Among these students, 98% are 25 years old or younger, 60% are women, 18% indicate an ethnicity other than White (4% African American/non-Hispanic; 1% Native American; 4% Asian or Pacific Islander; 8% Hispanic; 1% other), and 62% live on campus. Dedicated to creating ideal student learning environments, the College employs 179 full-time instructional faculty, maintains a student to faculty ratio of 11:1, and limits course enrollment to a maximum of 39 students.

Institution Profile:

Winter Park, FL

Private, Four-Year

3,829

Hybrid

Learning Community

The Seminar

The Rollins College Conference (RCC) is a hybrid seminar that blends extended orientation into approximately 30 discipline-linked courses on various topics. All first-year students are required to enroll in one of these courses, for which they receive four semester hours of credit. The course fulfills a general education requirement and is taught mostly by full-time faculty.

Initiated 11 years ago, the RCC program has the following aims: (a) to introduce students to academic life, (b) to develop a sense of community, and (c) to continue orientation throughout the fall semester. Several aspects of the program are also worth noting:

- RCC courses are designed both to focus on academic material and develop academic skills. Several classes are introductions to disciplines, but most are themed courses (e.g., Cultures in Conflict, Watery Pursuits, and Hispanic Experience in the US).
- Class enrollments do not exceed 16 students, and courses are discussion oriented.
- RCC instructors serve as students' academic advisors throughout the first year and until the students choose a major.

- In addition to meeting three times a week, the RCC also includes a special "4th hour" that meets Friday afternoons. This 4th hour provides students with opportunities for community building, continuing orientation, attending campus-wide events, and participating in a variety of community engagement projects.
- Two specially trained upperclass peer mentors serve as academic and social models for each course. The mentors regularly communicate with RCC students outside class and work with faculty to plan 4th hour activities.

A new living-learning program, open to about 20% of incoming students, was created in 2003. Two groups of students were involved and lived close to each other in a residence hall. One group consisted of honors students taking identical sections of a team-developed seminar. The second group consisted of students enrolled in three RCC courses that were thematically linked. The aim of these living-learning communities (LLCs) is to further enhance academic achievement and social engagement among students.

Research Design

One way Rollins assesses RCC outcomes is with Educational Benchmarking Incorporated's First-Year Initiative (FYI) Assessment. The FYI Assessment allows Rollins to compare outcomes (i.e., by Carnegie classification, a self-selected group of six colleges, and all FYI Assessment participants). Also, because this is Rollins' second year to use the FYI Assessment, trends showing improved outcomes are beginning to emerge. Further, since Rollins began the LLC endeavor in fall 2003, a series of independent samples t-tests has compared FYI Assessment outcomes of Rollins students enrolled in living-learning sections of the RCC with outcomes of students enrolled in traditional RCC sections. Of the 422 Rollins students who completed the FYI Assessment in fall 2003, 91 students (22%) were in LLC sections and 331 students (78%) were in traditional sections.

Findings

FYI Assessment results from the past two years have provided a way to monitor improvements related to social engagement, specifically survey items related to the factor of improved connections with peers. The table below suggests marked improvement in percentile rank overall from 2002 to 2003 for this factor, as just one example of overall social engagement improvements at Rollins (see Table 1).

Table 1 demonstrates an overall improvement in social engagement in all RCC classes, but we are making this category a special focus for the LLCs in the second year.

Table 1
Perceptions of Seminar Impact on Social Engagement, Fall 2002 and 2003 Cohorts

FYI Factor: Course Improved Connection with Peers	2002 Percentile ($N = 406$)	2003 Percentile ($N = 422$)
Course improved efforts to get to know students in my classes	44	73
Course improved ability to meet new people with common interests	35	61
Course improved ability to establish close relationships with peers	62	75
Overall factor	49	69

Additional evidence regarding the quality of the RCC at Rollins derives from an analysis of students who are part of the LLC endeavor. Independent samples *t*-tests indicated that LLC students were more likely than non-living-learning community students to agree with nine items on the FYI (Table 2). Moreover, the LLC responses were statistically the same regardless of whether the student was enrolled in an honors section or a thematically linked section of the RCC.

Table 2
Comparison of Course Outcomes for Living-Learning and Traditional Sections, Fall 2003 ($N = 422$)

FYI Item	LLC ($n = 91$)	Non-LLC ($n = 331$)	Difference
Course improved oral communication skills	5.264	4.441	.823
Course improved ability to see multiple sides of issues	5.923	4.941	.982
Course improved identifying solutions for complex problems	5.258	4.346	.912
Course improved evaluating the quality of opinions and facts	5.560	4.824	.736
Course increased understanding of the grading system	5.178	4.491	.687
Course experience included meaningful class discussions	5.978	5.112	.866
Course experience included productive use of classroom time	5.637	4.915	.722
Course experience included encouragement to speak in class	6.055	5.391	.664
Course readings were relevant	5.956	5.261	.695

Note. Responses for each item ranged from 1 (not at all) to 7 (significantly).

$p < .001$

Most of these responses fall within two categories: (a) improved higher cognitive skills and (b) an engaged classroom. They also point to achieved academic gains. LLC students were also significantly more likely than non-LLC students ($p < .05$) to report gains or improvement in the following areas as a result of taking the course:

- Decision-making skills
- Reviewing class notes before the next class meeting
- Seeking feedback from instructors
- Understanding registration procedures
- Understanding the role of my academic advisor
- Understanding how to obtain a tutor
- Understanding college students' sexual issues

These students were also more likely to say that the readings and subject matter were interesting and that the course had meaningful homework.

Because of the positive impact associated with LLCs, Rollins is expanding that program to include nearly one-third of all entering first-year students in fall 2004. If the impact of LLCs is significant after another year of analysis, Rollins may provide opportunities for all first-year students to participate in LLCs by fall 2005 or fall 2006. With early results showing increased social engagement and academic achievement for first-year students, Rollins now has evidence that it has created a distinctive first-year program worthy of emulation.

Contact

Hoyt L. Edge
Hugh F. and Jeannette G. McKean Chair and
Associate Dean of the Faculty
Rollins College
1000 Holt Avenue; Box 2749
Winter Park, FL 32789-4499
Phone: (407) 646-2280
Fax: (407) 646-2445
E-mail: hedge@rollins.edu

Additional Contributors:
James C. Eck
Assistant Provost for Institutional Research and Assessment

Sharon M. Carrier
Assistant Provost for Planning and Special Projects

Southeastern Louisiana University

The Institution

Southeastern Louisiana University, a four-year public institution, is located in Hammond, Louisiana, approximately 50 miles north of New Orleans. Of the 15,000 students enrolled, approximately 97% are from Louisiana, 89% commute, and more than 75% work. The student body is primarily female (65%), with 19% of the total representing minority populations (15% African American, 2% Hispanic, 2% other). While 35% are first-generation students (i.e., neither parent attended college), almost as many (37%) report having parents with a bachelor's degree or higher. Seventy-seven percent of the students are traditional students (under age 25).

The Seminar

Freshman Seminar 101 (FS 101) has been offered since 1997 as an elective course providing three hours of graded academic credit. The current program, replacing a one-hour course that had been in existence since 1987, is an academic seminar with generally uniform content across sections. Approximately one fourth of the entering first-year students elect to enroll in sections limited to 25 students. Recently, learning communities and various sections for specific populations such as scholarship recipients, athletes, and business majors have been created. Faculty members are full-time instructors in the Department of General Studies; however, occasionally courses are taught by a student affairs professional or outside faculty member.

The course is grounded in the theories of Astin and Tinto, attempting to encourage student success through academic and social integration. The basic goals are to (a) improve student success as measured by retention and progress to degree, (b) ease the transition by making students aware of University expectations such as information in the catalog and the importance of both academic and social involvement, (c) orient students to campus resources and facilities, (d) develop essential academic skills, and (e) increase student-student and student-faculty interaction.

Institution Profile:

Hammond, LA

Public, Four-Year

15;662

Academic w/Uniform

Content

Learning Community

135

Peer mentoring is a central component of the course and focuses on student health and safety. Peer mentors receive certification through Bacchus and Gamma, an international peer education program focusing on these issues. Faculty recommend previous Freshman Seminar students to become peer educators. Although training occurs in numerous ways, peer mentors learn core skills such as listening and confrontation, presentation skills, and stress management by working with faculty and staff at a weekend retreat. Student and faculty evaluations of the peer mentors are always positive.

Research Design

The purpose of this study was to compare the retention and progression rates for first-time, full-time, first-year students in FS 101 to the retention and progression rates for a matched cohort. Students in the comparison group were matched with the FS 101 students on race, gender, ACT composite score, and full-time versus part-time status. The matched group did not take FS 101. Students in initial cohorts were tracked from fall 2000 through fall 2003. A second purpose was to determine if the FS 101 students' study skills improved—one of the goals of the course. This was measured in a pre-/post-test design using the *Learning and Study Skills Inventory (LASSI)*, an 80-item assessment of students' use of learning and study strategies related to abilities, motivation, and self-regulation.

Findings

Table 1 provides the initial cohort numbers as well as the progress/retention rates for FS 101 students and a matched cohort. Seminar participants in all three cohorts consistently returned at a higher rate after one year (fall 2002), two years (fall 2001), and three years (fall 2000). They also progressed at a higher rate, meaning they earned 60 hours by the end of year two (sophomore level) or 90 hours by the end of year three (junior level). While chi-square analyses revealed a significant difference between the FS 101 students and the matched cohort in whether or not they were retained in their second year for fall 2002 [$\chi^2(1) = 7.18, p < .01$] and fall 2001 [$\chi^2(1) = 4.07, p < .05$], the difference for the fall 2000 cohort was not significant.

Study Skills

Using dependent samples *t*-tests, a comparison of pre- and post-test scores on the *LASSI* revealed a significant increase in Freshman Seminar students' study skills in all areas with the exception of the scales measuring motivation and attitude (See Table 2). Overall, the Freshman Seminar students experienced decreased anxiety even though the post-test was administered the week before

Table 1
Analysis of Student Retention and Progress to Degree

Fall 2000 initial cohort	FS 101 students ($n = 334$)		Matched cohort ($n = 333$)	
	Number	Percentage	Number	Percentage
Fall 2001 retention	224	67.1	206	61.9
Progress to degree	89	26.2	69	20.7
Fall 2002 retention	180	53.9	159	47.7
Progress to degree	58	17.4	48	14.4
Fall 2003 retention	154	46.1	136	40.8
Progress to degree	47	14.1	44	13.2
Fall 2001 initial cohort	($n = 396$)		($n = 395$)	
	Number	Percentage	Number	Percentage
Fall 2002 retention*	285	72.0	258	65.3
Progress to degree	104	26.3	93	23.5
Fall 2003 retention	221	55.8	213	53.9
Progress to degree	70	17.7	63	15.9
Fall 2002 initial cohort	($n = 469$)		($n = 463$)	
	Number	Percentage	Number	Percentage
Fall 2003 retention**	328	71.5	286	63.1
Progress to degree	122	26.1	95	21.0

Note. Progress to degree was defined as earning 60 hours after year two and 90 hours after year three.
*$p < .05$
**$p < .01$

final exams, when anxiety is typically high. Additional interventions might be considered to address attitude and motivation issues.

Conclusion

The assessment data provides important information for university administrators in decision-making positions. We believe that the success of our program can be attributed to the major academic focus, full-time faculty housed in an academic department, and peer educators. Currently, plans are underway to expand the benefits of the student, peer, and faculty relationships through various avenues including web-based discussion groups and class reunions.

Table 2

LASSI: Changes in Student Skills Fall 2003 Cohort (N = 300)

Scale	Mean pre-test	Mean post-test
Anxiety**	23.90	25.30
Attitude	31.44	30.75
Concentration***	24.23	25.70
Information processing***	25.68	28.20
Motivation	30.14	30.64
Self-testing***	23.88	25.66
Main ideas***	25.66	27.85
Study aids***	23.09	24.60
Time management*	22.38	23.25
Test strategies***	27.20	28.65

*p < .05
**p < .01
***p < .001

Contact

Frances B. Wood
Department Head, General Studies
Box 10576
Southeastern Louisiana University
Hammond, LA 70401
Phone: (985) 549-5682
Fax: (985) 549-5111

Additional Contributors:
Gwen Autin
Assistant Professor

Michelle Hall
Director, Institutional Research and Assessment

Southwest Missouri State University

The Institution

Southwest Missouri State University is a public, four-year institution and multi-campus system. At the main campus in Springfield, approximately 15,700 undergraduate students are enrolled. Of these students, nearly 77.4% are first-time, first-year students. Demographic data for the 2002-2003 academic year include an average first-year student composite ACT score of 23.1 and an average high school GPA of 2.72. Eighty-three percent of the student body is between the ages of 17 and 23, with 13.6% of the undergraduate population classified as first-generation students. The student body is slightly more female (55%) than male and is composed of mostly in-state students (91%). The racial and ethnic makeup of the student body is largely White/Non-Hispanic (88.2%), followed by 2.4% African American, 1.2% Hispanic, 1.3% Asian/Pacific Islander, .9% Native American, 2.1% non-resident alien, and 3.9% unknown.

The Seminar

Introduction to University Life (IDS 110) is an academic seminar with generally uniform content across sections. The course was piloted in fall 1994 as an elective on a Pass/Not Pass grading basis. In fall 1995, it became a graded general education requirement for all incoming first-year students (with the exception of transfer students and those entering with 24 semester credit hours or more earned beyond high school graduation). Approximately 88% of first-year students enroll in the course. For this one-credit course, students meet for two 50-minute periods a week; the sections are capped at 25 students each. Dedicated classrooms have armchairs arranged in a circle (to enhance class bonding and unity as well as easy rearrangement of chairs for small-group work). Faculty teach approximately 60% of the sections; administrators, support staff, and graduate assistants teach the remaining sections. A peer leadership component (sophomores, juniors, and seniors who assist the teachers and the first-year students in the course) was added in fall 1996; approximately 40% of the sections have a peer leader.

Institution Profile:

Springfield, MO

Public, Four-Year

18,930

Academic w/Uniform

Content

The mission of the course is to facilitate the transition to university life and assist students in achieving academic success. The goals are to present opportunities for students to develop responsibility and self-awareness, to explore the academic environment at the university, to develop personal support, and to plan for the future. Major topics covered for the course include:

- Orientation to college
- Effective communication skills
- Time management and setting priorities
- Identification and application of personal learning style
- Reading, listening, note-taking, and test-taking skills
- Academic decision making
- Health and wellness
- Personal responsibility
- Computers use and technology
- Library research
- Writing and speaking skills
- Positive relationships
- Career planning
- Campus involvement
- Money management
- Diversity

Course functions and activities to support the mission and goals have been developed for all sections. Teachers participate in a 1½-day training workshop in April and a kick-off meeting the week before classes begin. Case studies give students the opportunity to develop critical-thinking skills and to participate in small groups. Videotapes have been produced on topics such as The Writing Center, Career Services, and Becoming Involved on Campus. All sections participate in large-group presentations on alcohol and drug abuse; sexually transmitted diseases, including HIV; and abuse and sexual assault prevention. Two sections at a time go to the library computer lab for hands-on training in conducting electronic searches.

Research Design

In addition to tracking retention rates as a measurement of course success, a survey instrument was designed to determine the factors most significant to first-year success. In particular, we looked at academic success as measured by GPA. Beginning in fall 1995, students enrolled in the college success course completed the Survey of Freshmen questionnaire (a 54-item instrument) within the final two weeks of the term. Questions asked about students' academic load, study hours, employment, class attendance, sleep, nutrition, academic advisement, use of campus resources, spiritual practice, and involvement in campus activities.

Instructors were required to take attendance each class period and to report the number of absences for each student at the end of the term. The attendance factor was added individually to each student's computer score sheet. After the grades had been reported, the surveys were processed by computer services.

The tabulated summaries of responses enabled the institution to observe trends—comparing the most recent term with those of previous years and comparing the average fall semester first-year students with that of the spring semester. Beginning in 1997, cross correlations were made to determine which factors (according to the Pearson .05 level of significance) had the most positive impact on students' GPA achievement. The student response rate (willingness to participate and produce usable questionnaires) was 98%.

Findings

Retention Rates

Before the college success course was implemented in 1995, the retention rate of all first-year students was 62.4%. In fall 2003, the retention rate of all first-year students who completed the college success course was 81.3%; those who did not complete the course had a 17.6 % retention rate. First-year students who did not enroll in the college success course (including transfer students not required to take the course) had a 64.8% retention rate.

Survey of Freshmen

For each of the last five years, the Survey of Freshmen results (cross correlations) have identified factors that were statistically significant (at the .05 level using Pearson's correlation) for academic achievement as measured by GPA. The highest course grades, semester GPAs, and cumulative GPAs were earned by students whose practices were among those described below:

- *Course load.* Students who carried at least 15 credit hours a term achieved higher GPAs than full-time students who carried 12 credit hours and part-time students.
- *Study hours.* Those who reported studying at least two hours outside class for every one hour in class earned the highest GPAs.
- *Employment.* Working at a job no more than 20 hours a week did not have an effect on GPA, but employment hours over 20 hours a week had a negative impact on GPA.

- *Class attendance.* Students who attended classes regularly with no more than one absence per term in a course achieved the highest GPAs.
- *Sleep.* Students who slept seven to eight hours a night earned the highest GPAs.
- *Nutrition.* Students who reported eating three nutritious meals a day earned the best grades.
- *Academic advisement.* Students with the highest GPAs reported the most positive experiences with academic advisement.
- *Campus resources.* Use of three campus resources had a significant impact on students' GPAs: (a) computer lab, (b) campus library, and (c) writing center.
- *Spiritual practices.* Students who regularly attended or participated in a religious center—on or off campus—had the highest GPAs.
- *Campus activities.* Students who participated in out-of-class activities or events achieved better grades. They were more committed to returning to college the next year and to graduating within five years.

While many of these factors do not relate to participation in the seminar course, the course curriculum and textbook do emphasize these as key strategies for supporting academic success. These strategies are also shared with all academic support departments on campus. Instead of lecturing and giving advice, the teachers and peer leaders present these results as "last year's first-year students are sharing with you the factors that supported their earning top grades." Built within the time management unit are the course load, study hours, and employment factors. Important to the study skills and test-taking preparation units are the factors on study hours, class attendance, sleep, and nutrition. The health and wellness unit highlights the factors on nutrition, sleep, campus activities, and spiritual practice. While the use of all campus resources is encouraged, support in using the three that have the most impact on students' grades (i.e., computer lab, campus library, and writing center) are emphasized.

Results from the Survey of Freshmen helped support decisions on the course design and development, videotape production, large-group presentations, textbook selection, and content of training workshops for teachers and for peer leaders. The academic advisors refer to the findings as they discuss scheduling and other academic decisions with their advisees. Sharing the results with decision makers across campus has helped gain respect and support for the course.

Contact

Mona Casady, Professor
Management Department
Southwest Missouri State University
901 South National Avenue
Springfield MO 65804
Phone: (417) 836-4340
Fax: (417) 836-3004
E-mail: MonaCasady@smsu.edu

State University of New York at Brockport

The Institution

The State University of New York (SUNY) at Brockport is a public, four-year, comprehensive, liberal arts college with a significant investment in accredited professional and graduate programs. The institution, located in Brockport, New York, has an average annualized FTE base of 7,054 and a yearly first-year student class of approximately 1,000. The College is predominantly residential (on-campus) for first-year students, but a higher proportion of non-first-year students live off campus. SUNY Brockport draws a number of commuter students from the Rochester metropolitan area and surrounding towns. Within the undergraduate population, 58% are female; the racial/ethnic composition is approximately 79% White, 5% African American, 2% Hispanic, 1% Asian American, 1% foreign students, less than 1% Native American, and 11% unknown/not reported.

The Seminar

The College's first-year seminar, *Academic Planning Seminar* (APS), serves as an extended orientation to college. This offering and its predecessor entitled *Dimensions of Liberal Education* have been taught for more than 20 years. The course is required for all students who enter the College with fewer than 24 credits. Students completing the course earn one liberal arts credit. Usually there are 22 or fewer students in each section. Approximately 80% of the first-year class is enrolled in the course. The College runs at least 48 sections (most in the fall semester) taught by full-time faculty and professional staff. Instructors receive a $1,000 honorarium.

The *Academic Planning Seminar* includes the following goals:

- To provide regular contact with a faculty/staff member who cares about student's progress
- To give students a better understanding of their instructors' expectations

Institution Profile:

Brockport, NY

Public, Four-Year

6,962

Extended Orientation

- To help students develop a supportive peer group
- To assist students with time management
- To introduce students to the College's Career Services office and help them understand their options for majors and careers
- To explain the College's General Education program and the importance of a liberal arts education
- To introduce students to the College's Student Learning Center services
- To assist students in learning to use the College library
- To increase the students' understanding of cultural, racial, and sexual diversity
- To improve awareness of health/wellness issues
- To help improve note taking, textbook reading, and examination taking skills
- To increase student appreciation of cultural experiences (e.g., art, dance, theater)
- To introduce students to important College policies on registration, drop/add, and withdrawal

Research Design

SUNY Brockport's *Academic Planning Seminar* is evaluated by a questionnaire administered to students in the individual course sections using a scannable custom form. The questionnaire evaluates the course goals and requires students to make two evaluations: (a) the degree to which each course goal is perceived as important and (b) the degree to which each particular course goal was achieved through APS. A five-point Likert scale is used in both measures.

Findings

Data collected from all sections are pooled (more than 700 students each year) and reported as the percent of total respondents choosing each alternative on the Likert scales. Table 1 presents students' positive responses to course goals for academic years beginning in 2001 and 2002.

Of all the course goals, students show most interest in "understanding career options." This is to be expected as students enter college with careers on their minds but often have little experience in what their career options actually are. Interestingly, knowing about the College's Career Services office, the students' major source of specific information about careers, is considered much less important. The orientation goals of understanding instructors' expectations, college policies, and having regular contact with a faculty/staff member were also rated high in importance. Students seem to understand the importance of these goals in helping them negotiate the college environment successfully.

Table 1

Students Identifying First-Year Seminar Course Goals as Important and Accomplished (in percentages)

APS Course Goal	2001		2002	
	Importance	Accomplished	Importance	Accomplished
Helped me understand some possible career options	74	64	85	81
Helped me understand instructors' expectations	72	66	75	69
Provided regular contact with a faculty member who cares about my progress	71	68	75	76
Informed me about drop/add, withdrawal, and registration policies	70	67	78	79
Helped me understand the Brockport General Education program	67	69	82	84
Helped me manage my time	65	55	70	55
Helped me improve my note taking, textbook reading, and examination taking skills	62	46	64	43
Helped me understand how to use the College library	61	60	67	59
Introduced me to the services at the Student Learning Center	50	64	60	75
Introduced me to the services of the Career Services Office	48	58	58	68
Helped me develop a supportive peer group	47	44	53	50
Helped me form a broader perspective on cultural, racial, and sexual diversity	46	44	49	37
Increased my awareness of health/wellness	46	35	52	47
Helped me increase my appreciation for cultural experiences (e.g., art, dance, theatre)	39	40	34	33

Note. Data points were obtained by adding the percentages of students choosing the two most positive categories on the five-point Likert scale.

On the negative side, the students generally rate being exposed to diversity, health/wellness issues, and cultural experiences in the arts as least important to them. They also report a low perception of accomplishment of these same goals. Instructors may need to spend more time informing students of the importance of these subjects. Students were also less convinced that the goals of learning to manage time and improve study skills were accomplished in proportion to their perceived importance. The introductions to the Student Learning Center and the Career Services office were accomplished to a degree that exceeded the student perception of their importance.

The survey showed a high degree of student satisfaction with their APS instructors as persons with whom they would be comfortable discussing personal issues and as sources of academic advice (Table 2). This is a major orientation goal and is viewed as very important in student retention.

Table 2
Student Satisfaction with APS Course and Instructor (in percentages)

	2001-2002	2002-2003
APS was important in helping me adjust to my first semester	66	65
I was comfortable discussing personal issues with APS instructor	75	73
I was pleased with APS instructor as source of academic advice	79	81

Investigations such as the present study are important in identifying the course goals that students value most highly. It is obviously important to retain those elements in a successful first-year seminar course. The identification of goals that students think are less important can help instructors understand student resistance to working on these goals. Faculty generally think that goals such as introducing students to cultural experiences in the arts and to diversity are important parts of the liberal education. Students do not always agree. The challenge in this case is how to structure experiences that can influence students to think more positively about these topics as experiences that can enrich their lives.

Contact

P. Michael Fox
Vice Provost for Academic Affairs
SUNY College at Brockport
618 Allen Administration Building
350 New Campus Drive
Brockport, NY 14420
Phone: (585) 395-2504
Fax: (585) 395-2006
E-mail: mfox@brockport.edu

Additional Contributor:
Marcella Esler
Assistant to the Vice President for Enrollment Management,
Director of Student Retention

Temple University

The Institution

Located in Philadelphia, Pennsylvania, Temple University is a comprehensive, public research university that enrolls more than 33,000 students, 21,640 of whom are undergraduates. According to the fall 2003 student profile, Temple enrolled 3,778 first-time, first-year students. Between 1998 and 2003, Temple's undergraduate enrollment skyrocketed by 28% to 21,640 students. That increase was accompanied by a significant rise in the credentials of entering students. Average combined SAT scores increased from 1020 to 1088. The average high school GPA was 3.25 on a 4.00 scale. More than half of all entering first-year students now reside on campus and nearly one third of Temple's undergraduates live in University housing, facilities developed in partnership with the University, or in private residences near campus. Temple has a diverse student population: 59% of the students are White, 18% African American, 10% Asian American, 3% Hispanic, .3% Native American, and 8% report "other." Approximately 43% of students are female.

The Seminar

Learning for the New Century is a one-credit, elective student success course open to any student at Temple University. The seminar is a combination of the "extended orientation" and "basic study skills" models. Half of the sections are included in linked-course learning communities. When the seminar is linked to a learning community, it takes on the additional characteristics of an academic seminar that explores the interdisciplinary themes across the courses in the community.

The course meets for 11 weeks in the fall semester. Students receive a letter grade and the credit applies towards graduation in all undergraduate programs. The first section was offered in 1995, and in 2004—the 10th year for the course—we will offer 25 sections with a total program enrollment of more than 600 students. Section enrollments vary from 17 to 40 students with

---

Institution Profile:

Philadelphia, PA

Public, Four-Year

33,286

Hybrid

Learning Community

most sections enrolling 20 to 25 students. In 2003, we piloted a section of the seminar that was team taught and enrolled 100 students who met once a week in lecture and once a week in a 20-student, peer-led recitation. Seminars are taught by a faculty member, administrator, academic advisor, or student affairs professional partnered with an undergraduate peer teacher. The mission of the course is to recognize where students are in terms of their self-awareness and study skills and help them discover and practice the knowledge and skills necessary to grow academically and socially. The first-year seminar course goals are to:

- Enhance students' intellectual development and improve their study behaviors and skills
- Enhance students' social development and engagement in the campus community
- Promote collaborative learning and group work
- Allow students to practice technology applications and retrieval of information

In fall 2003, the course enrolled 599 students, with females comprising 67% of the enrollments. In terms of ethnicity, 60% reported White, 22% African American, 7% Asian, 2% Hispanic, and 9% reported "other." The average age of enrollees was 18, and nearly 70% lived on campus. Twenty-three percent were first-generation college students, reporting that neither their father nor mother attended college. The combined, average SAT score for seminar students was 1050.

Learning for the New Century is one of four first-year seminars offered at Temple University. The Fox School of Business and Management, School of Communications and Theater, and College of Science and Technology offer college-based seminars that focus on transition to college and learning in the disciplines. Total seminar enrollment for all four versions is approximately 40% of all entering first-year students.

Research Design

Each fall, the course is evaluated using both quantitative and qualitative methods. In fall 2001 and 2002, the program administered the First-Year Initiative (FYI) Assessment. In 2003, the program administered Temple University's new Course and Teaching Evaluation (CATE). The CATE features 19 standard questions on the course, instruction, and student learning experience. The program includes 20 supplemental questions, adapted from the FYI Assessment, that were designed to gain feedback related to the goals, classroom environment, and content of the first-year seminar course. In addition to the end-of-semester course evaluations, the program regularly conducts reflective interviews with lead instructors and peer teachers. Teachers meet as a group to discuss their expectations for teaching a seminar, what they experienced, which approaches and activities did or did not work in their course, how they incorporated the summer reading selection and course text, and ways they might improve their course.

Findings

Participating in a first-year seminar increases students' understanding of Temple policies and procedures. Sixty-six percent of participants agreed that the course increased their understanding of course registration. Section means for this item were highest in classes taught by academic advisors. Sixty-nine percent agreed that the course increased their understanding of the importance of advising, and 73% indicated the course increased their understanding of how to obtain personal and academic assistance. The 2001 and 2002 FYI Assessment reports indicated that student perception of improved time and priorities management was an important predictor of satisfaction with the seminar. In 2003, 50% indicated that the course improved their ability to establish an effective study schedule, and 53% indicated the course improved their time management. More improvement is needed in this area.

The course promotes collaborative learning and group work. In class, students are comfortable asking questions and expressing their opinions. Eighty-nine percent of the students said their course provided opportunities for students to work together, and 70% said their course included meaningful class discussions.

The 2001 and 2002 FYI Assessment results also indicated that "engaging pedagogy" was a predictor of student satisfaction. Instructor training was revised to include more sessions on active learning, and on the 2003 evaluations, 80% of the respondents agreed that the course included a variety of teaching methods.

On the 2002 FYI Assessment, approachability and availability of the teachers was the highest overall mean. On the course evaluations, 86% of the students indicated that the instructors clearly stated course objectives, and 83% said instructors graded fairly. Seventy-two percent agreed that they received prompt feedback about their work, with 83% agreeing that teachers were organized and prepared for class.

Overall, students indicate that their experience at Temple has been positive. Eighty-one percent agreed they would recommend Temple to a friend, and 84% indicated they planned to return to Temple next fall.

End-of-semester interviews with instructors and peer teachers reveal useful information about class activities, course materials, and teacher training.

Teachers report using a variety of approaches to promote student participation: discussions, debates, small-group activities, and role-playing exercises. To integrate the course text, instructors use journal assignments, short reaction papers to an assigned question related to the book, quizzes, and class discussion. Most instructors assign at least one small group project and an oral presentation to promote collaborative learning and presentational speaking skills. Teachers find the instructor handbook, particularly the course guidelines and sample syllabus, useful in planning their sections. The opportunity to learn from experienced seminar instructors is one of the most highly evaluated aspects of the summer training workshop.

Contact

Jodi Levine Laufgraben
Associate Vice Provost
Temple University
301 Conwell Hall
1801 N. Broad Street
Philadelphia, PA 19122
Phone: (215) 204-7423
Fax: (215) 204-5862
E-mail: jodih@temple.edu

University of Bridgeport

The Institution

Located in Bridgeport, Connecticut, the University of Bridgeport is a private, non-sectarian, doctoral intensive university that promotes careers in an international context. Of its 3,400 students, 1,100 are undergraduate, roughly half of whom live on campus. Fifty-five percent of undergraduates are female and 19% are international. Students come from the following racial/ethnic backgrounds: 45.7% African American/non-Hispanic, 23.2% White/non-Hispanic, 14.0% Hispanic, 10.6% non-resident alien, 3.1% Asian/Pacific Islander, 1.0% Native American, and 3.4% undeclared/unknown.

The Seminar

The First-Year Studies Program serves as a bridge to traditional undergraduate majors for underprepared students (35% of entering undergraduates in 2003-2004). The Core Curriculum, required of all undergraduates in 33 major programs, inculcates skills for life-long learning and the academic value of an international perspective. The University Senate approved the addition of FYS 101 ("First-Year Seminar") to the undergraduate Core in 2003. FYS 101 is a required, three-credit hour course with an enrollment capacity of 20 students per section. Ten sections ran in fall 2003 and six in spring 2004, which afforded space to 320 first-year students. Nearly all (94%) first-year students enrolled in the seminar taught primarily by full-time faculty members using a common syllabus.

The primary goals of the course are to help students understand the academic culture at the University and to provide a context for adoption of this academic culture. Designed as a challenging academic seminar with universal content, FYS 101 focuses on the theme of overcoming cultural challenges. Adoption of academic culture is facilitated by pursuing goals that support the University's academic mission, such as helping students understand a variety of cultures and navigate the challenges when encountering cultures different from their own. Within this learning context,

Institution Profile:

Bridgeport, CT

Private, Four-Year

3,165

Academic w/Uniform

 Content

students are encouraged to develop foundational skills for subsequent study in the Core Curriculum and academic majors. The seminar helps students read perceptively, write persuasively, and speak confidently.

Instructors of FYS 101 facilitate active, participatory learning. Requirements include reading; maintaining a diary; writing reflection papers; and participating in plenary sessions, classroom discussions, and activities. Reading assignments (primarily short stories and essays) focus on understanding cultures, overcoming challenges, and grappling with issues of personal identity.

Instructors use a variety of approaches to help students grapple with assigned material. Some use small-group discussions with defined objectives that are later presented to the whole class. At other times, instructors use role playing, skit enactment, letter writing, in-class writing and paper revision, and a host of other learning strategies.

Research Design

Designed in-house, assessment instruments included quantitative and qualitative approaches. Scaled response pre- and post-seminar surveys and narrative questions measured the seminar's efficacy and students' experience in adopting the University's academic culture. Primary indicators were feelings about activities such as attending class or completing assignments and their perceived relevance for success in college. Also measured were motivational factors (i.e., self-concept and values) relevant to the University's academic culture. In each of the quantitative measures, students ranked items on a six-point Likert-type scale (no neutral), with 1 being "strongly like" and 6 being "strongly dislike." The data reported here reverses the scale in order to make the data shifts easier to understand. Higher numbers indicate movement toward the "strongly like" side of the continuum.

In addition, mid-term assessment using narrative surveys addressed pedagogical methods to improve the course as it proceeded. Interpretations were developed collegially. A questionnaire completed at the close of each semester gauged student reactions to assigned readings. FYS faculty meetings focused on qualitative assessment of the selected readings, classroom activities, and course policies. Conclusions from qualitative assessment prompted minor formative changes and provided summative direction for comprehensive course redesign for the second year. We continue to study the validity of the instruments.

Findings

Our findings indicate that students responded positively to the seminar. Feelings about academic activities (e.g., reading, writing, asking questions in class) were positively affected both semesters (Figure 1). The representative data summary chart below shows positive shifts in feelings about activities for the fall 2003 semester. On the (reversed) 1 - 6 scale, the average rank was $2.89 \pm .03$ at the beginning of the semester and $3.11 \pm .04$ at the semester's conclusion. This shift is significant according to standard error calculation (standard deviation [$sd = .38$ for beginning of semester data] divided by the square root of n [$n = 140$ for the beginning of the semester]). Though the gains are modest, the error bars, reported on the chart below, are small and do not overlap. The largest positive gains were observed in attitudes about writing papers (a particular focus of all instructors), about writing in general, and about taking a seminar class.

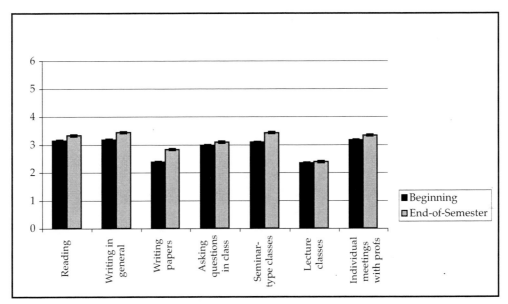

Figure 1. Student attitudes toward course activities, fall 2003.

An end-of-semester questionnaire gauged reactions to each of the reading assignments. It showed that students viewed 90% of the readings more favorably after classroom discussions. A range of 25% to 50% of students reported increased favor for different assignments. The power of FYS-specific classroom activities, which were designed to illuminate the readings, may explain this result. Narrative comments support this interpretation: Many students attributed the positive shift to direct engagement in the pedagogy of FYS (discussions, reflection, focused writing assignments). A representative comment came from one student, who reported, "I liked listening to the opinions of other students, because that helped me understand the readings." Yet another opined, "Small classes rule. I learned so much about the world from this small class."

We found that attitudes students ascribe to success in college (e.g., completing all assignments and attending class are good ideas) were not affected either semester. They were strong at the start and finish and notably stronger than feelings about doing academic activities. Average ranking for perceived relevance of activities to college success was 4.17 ± .03 at the beginning and 4.17 ± .05 at the semester's close. These results suggest that students who do not complete reading assignments hold values at variance with their actions. Hence, these students do not need to change their attitudes about assigned readings; they need to change their behaviors. The redesigned syllabus for fall 2004 will focus more on the academic culture of doing and less on academic culture as ideation.

Self-concept (i.e., whether students believe they are good at academic tasks such as reading, writing, and speaking) was not affected in the fall semester but showed statistically significant improvement in the spring semester. The average self-ratings on a six-point Likert-type scale for the beginning and ending of the fall semester were 3.72 ± .03 and 3.71 ± .03, respectively; the average self-ratings for the beginning and ending of the spring semester were 3.32 ± .04 and 3.56 ± .03, respectively. Thus, in the first semester, the seminar did not affect self-concept, but it did in the second semester.

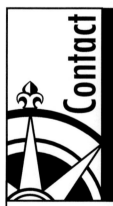

Contact

Stephen Healey
Chair, Core Commission
Director, World Religions Program
University of Bridgeport
126 Park Avenue
Bridgeport, CT 06601
Phone: (203) 576-4212
E-mail: healey@bridgeport.edu

Additional Contributors:
Jennifer Frederick
Assistant Professor of Chemistry
Western Connecticut State University

Timothy Eves
Assistant Professor of Humanities
Director of First Year Seminar

The University of Calgary

The Institution

The University of Calgary is a publicly funded doctoral research university serving approximately 29,000 students. Located in Calgary, Alberta, Canada, the University is primarily a commuter campus, particularly at the undergraduate level, although 18% of all students are from out of province and 6% are visa students. Slightly more than half (54%) of the students are female. No data are available on socioeconomic and ethnic status of students, but there are no indications of an above-average number of at-risk students. Withdrawal rate for first-year students stands at approximately 15%.

The Seminar

The University of Calgary offers first-year programs on a college-by-college basis. The Faculty of Communication and Culture, an interdisciplinary college that attracts a higher than usual proportion of undecided first-year students, is the only college to offer limited enrollment first-year seminars with variable academic content. The course, *General Studies 201: First-Year Inquiry Seminar* (GNST 201), is a one-semester course offering the equivalent of three units of general option credit. It is highly recommended for all students in the college, and each section enrolls 25 students. In 2004-05, the course will serve 275 students on a first-come, first-served basis. This represents only 10% of the college's total first-year enrollment, but this percentage is expected to rise as institution-wide changes relieve the faculty of disproportionate responsibility for undecided entering students. The course has been taught in its present form since 1999.

GNST 201 is designed not simply to improve persistence, but also to improve students' engagement with the academic life of the University. Tenure-track faculty, who select a topic related to their research interests and tailor it to be accessible to first-year students, teach the course.

Institution Profile:

Calgary, Alberta, Canada

Public, Four-Year

28,869

Academic w/Variable Content

A central pedagogical strategy is a term-long project on a topic chosen by the student, broken into a series of sub-projects such as proposal, working bibliography, reflective journal, summaries, drafts, and other projects that cumulate toward a final research paper. This project allows students to both build academic skills and acquire (relatively) deep familiarity with the topic area in ways that are impossible with the typical rushed term paper. The extended project promotes intellectual investment in the research process and allows for the mistakes, roadblocks, and topic reassessments that are a necessary part of "real" research.

Research Design

All students complete an exit survey. The fall 2003 class was also surveyed to determine whether students who had taken GNST 201 showed differences in key attitudes to learning compared to students who had not. Finally, a sample of 19 students from the fall 2004 class was studied through intensive semi-structured interviews to determine their attitudes toward research and their awareness of research processes.

Findings

On the exit survey, students rated the course 5.5 on a seven-point scale for helping them become more comfortable with the academic environment of the university and rated the inquiry-based structure of the course as 5.5. Students reported that the most important skill acquired was the ability to find resources, followed by writing, reading, speaking, and collaborating with others. Narrative comments highlighted the small class size, interaction with library staff, and opportunity for guided independent research as the best features of the course. A few reported being uncomfortable with the amount of independent work required, which these students did not define as "teaching."

The comparative survey suggests that students who take GNST 201, compared with other first-year Communication and Culture students who do not, were more comfortable speaking to professors, using the library, and adapting in general to the university environment. They also rate collaborative work more positively. Overall, however, they are more negative in their response to the prompts "I think I am learning more by being in a research-based university rather than a college or technical school" and "I feel comfortable with my ability to find answers to questions even if my professor does not tell me directly." The low response rate (< 12%) means that this data is not statistically reliable. However, the survey does suggest that, although the course is generally achieving its goals, students' intense immersion in university-level research may be making them less, rather than more, comfortable with the research-based environment and with inquiry-based learning (that is, finding their own answers). This may simply reflect a transitional stage in the students' personal development. However, it suggests that the course should focus more strongly on providing support for independent work to help students gain confidence.

The qualitative survey reveals that students taking the course place an extremely high value on being able to choose their own research topics and to pursue a topic over an extended time. They report feeling a great deal of satisfaction in starting with a general area of study and gradually focusing it to a specific question relevant to their own interests and life experience. They also report a much higher level of one-to-one engagement with the professor than in most other courses, even when those courses are of a similar size. Their descriptions of their research also indicate a more sophisticated process and a higher level of engagement in GNST 201 assignments compared with research projects in other first-year courses. In GNST 201, students are more likely to return to the library a number of times as their research questions deepen, seek a wide range of sources of information, write exploratory drafts, receive formative feedback from the professor and peers, and integrate primary and secondary sources into an argument rather than merely reporting information.

However, the students interviewed still have only a hazy idea of how knowledge is produced and circulated in the academic environment. They see the purpose of references exclusively as a means of protecting against charges of plagiarism rather than, as their professors see it, as a means of inviting others to trace back the same intellectual currents. In a related finding, only one student of the 19 reports having found information by following a reference rather than by searching from scratch, and only two can explain with reasonable clarity how journals work and how and why the information they contain gets there. Overall, this study suggests that the course is enhancing students' academic engagement but that more attention could be paid to the ways in which the academic system works as a knowledge-making community.

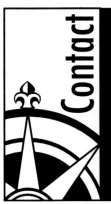

Contact

Doug Brent
Professor and Associate Dean (Academic)
Faculty of Communication and Culture
University of Calgary
2500 University Drive NW
Calgary, AB, Canada
T2N 1N4
Phone: (403) 220-5458
Fax: (403) 282-6716
E-mail: dabrent@ucalgary.ca

University of Colorado at Colorado Springs

The Institution

The University of Colorado at Colorado Springs (UCCS), one of three campuses in the University of Colorado System, is a public four-year institution with 7,800 undergraduate and graduate students. Approximately 900 students are residential. Nearly two thirds of UCCS students are female, and almost 23% percent are ethnic minorities, including 8% Hispanic, 5.0% Asian American, 4.0% African American, 1.5% international, 1% Native American, and 3.0% unknown. Only 20% of first-time, first-year students are "traditional" students (i.e., those who are first-generation college students, earn a high-school diploma, enroll full-time immediately after finishing high school, depend on parents for financial support, and either do not work during the school year or work part-time).

The Seminar

In Interdepartmental Studies (ID) 101 (Freshman Seminar), college success skills are infused into student-centered, team-taught, three-credit, elective academic seminars with variable content. Eight multiple-section, thematic, first-year courses are created by cross-college teams of three to five faculty: (a) *Life and Death* (service-learning intensive; each first-year student is paired with an "elder companion" in the city), (b) *Mating Game*, (c) *American Dream*, (d) *Unreality*, (e) *Street Beat*, (f) *ColoradoLiving.com* (field-trip intensive), (g) *Driven*, and (h) *Crime and Punishment*. Each week, the course topic is examined from a different disciplinary perspective, thereby introducing students to various majors and professors. Faculty teams create course content to meet students' personal, academic, and community goals by weaving their own disciplines together and inviting additional faculty to represent other relevant disciplines. In each topical course, students in sections of 15 work on four skill sets to enhance college and career success: (a) speaking and listening, (b) writing and reading, (c) teamwork, and (d) technology. The course begins two full days before other classes during "Preview Daze," which counts as five weeks of class. The course continues for the next 11 weeks. During the early start-up, ID 101 students receive the faculty's undivided attention, participate in technology training in campus computer labs, go off campus for service-learning trips, and bond with both faculty and one another. When the regular term begins, the course meets once a week for three hours in residence hall space. During the first half of each class session, all students in a topic group come together for "common time" (a presentation or activity) in a large room. During the second half, each faculty member and junior teaching assistant work closely with 15 students in a small seminar room close by. The course began in fall 1991 with a single section of 16 students, and currently serves half of the entering first-year class or more than 500 students.

Research Design

Typically reserved for academic disciplines, our full Academic Program Review included writing a self-study document with major sections on the history of the program; current status of the program with regard to teaching, research/creative work, and university/community service; resources; diversity; student outcome assessment (a statistical package prepared by the Office of Institutional Research); annual faculty retreat agendas; newspaper articles; faculty curricula vitae; syllabi; and sample course planning materials. The review also included external evaluations by two reviewers, prominent in the first-year experience movement, who conducted a site visit. External reviewers met with faculty who teach in the program, undergraduate junior teaching assistants, first-year students who had taken the course, and faculty adversaries from outside the program.

Findings

The Office of Institutional Research prepared a comprehensive statistical package comparing seminar and non-seminar students on a variety of relevant measures. Analysis of the 1998 cohort revealed that seminar students persisted in their college careers at a higher rate than non-seminar students (Figure 1).

Further analysis of fall-to-fall retention rates for cohorts 1997 to 2001 revealed higher persistence rates among seminar students when compared to non-seminar students. Although longitudinal analysis for cohort persistence rates has not been completed for the 2002 cohort and beyond, we have noted that seminar students continue to persist at higher rates than non-seminar students.

Measures of academic success, noted by the students' GPA at the end of the first year, further indicate that seminar students, on average, earn higher GPAs than non-seminar students (2.78 vs. 2.66, respectively). No statistically signifi-

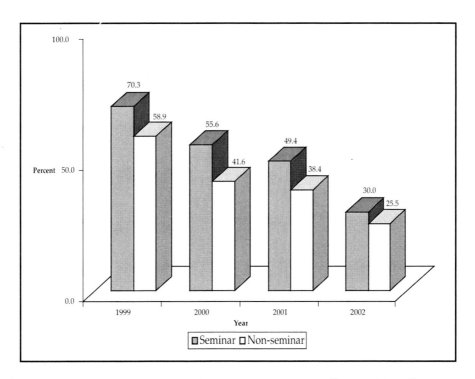

Figure 1. First-year seminar student persistence in college, 1998 cohort. Seminar participants persisted at significantly higher levels in 1999 and 2000 (*p* < .05) and in 2001 and 2002 (*p* < .01).

cant differences were found between seminar participants and their non-seminar counterparts on three entry variables: (a) high school rank, (b) ACT scores, and (c) SAT scores. In fact, despite lower scores on the ACT (22.3 seminar vs. 23.1 non-seminar average score), consistently lower entry scores on the SAT, and nearly equivalent high school rankings (69.5 seminar vs. 68.3 non-seminar average rank), seminar students consistently persisted, completed more credit hours, earned higher grades, and graduated at higher rates than their non-seminar counterparts.

Results of our in-house 2001 New First-Year Student Survey (Cronbach's alpha = .87) helped us compare responses between seminar students and non-seminar students to questions exploring 11 variables. Of these variables, six were statistically significant at a 95% confidence level: (a) communication skills, (b) use of campus resources, (c) relationships with faculty, (d) adjustment to college, (e) technology skills, and (f) integration into campus community.

Contact

Constance Staley
Professor of Communication and Director,
Freshman Seminar Program
Department of Communication
PO Box 7150
University of Colorado at Colorado Springs
Colorado Springs, CO 80933-7150
Phone: (719) 262-4123
Fax: (719) 262-4030
E-mail: cstaley@uccs.edu

University of Delaware

The Institution

The University of Delaware (UD) is a four-year institution located in Newark, Delaware, with more than 16,000 undergraduate students, nearly 3,000 graduate students, and 1,000 faculty members. Undergraduates can choose from more than 100 academic majors. The University is a state-assisted, privately controlled institution. It is a residential campus with traditional students from diverse backgrounds and geographic regions. Fifty-eight percent of undergraduates are female, 85.6% are White, 5.5% are African American, 3.3% are Asian, 3.1% are Hispanic, 1% are non-resident alien, and 0.3% are Native American. The average age is 20.

The Seminar

University 101 (UNIV 101): *First-Year Experience* is an academic seminar covering various topics and is a required part of the LIFE (Learning Integrated Freshman Experience) program. LIFE is an academic living-learning experience for first-year college students, who form small learning communities organized around several of their academic courses, an academic theme, and out-of-class experiences integrating the courses and themes. A maximum of 16 students are enrolled in each cluster, and 15% of first-year students enroll in LIFE.

UNIV 101 is a one-credit, pass/fail course in which students will:

- Participate in a community of students with common interests and goals
- Become familiar with the University of Delaware and its various student resources
- Learn more about their field of interest through such activities as field trips, conversations with practitioners, and on- and off-campus programs
- Participate in a group-based project that will allow them to apply what they have learned in the cluster courses to the real world

> **Institution Profile:**
>
> Newark, DE
>
> Public, Four-Year
>
> 21,121
>
> Academic w/Variable
>
> Content
>
> Learning Community

- Reflect on their own learning process and their goals
- Refine their academic and communication skills necessary for a successful college experience

Each cluster has a peer mentor, an advanced undergraduate student, who facilitates UNIV 101 and helps students adjust to the academic life of the University.

Each cluster also has a faculty contact, typically the instructor for one of the two academic courses of the LIFE cluster. The faculty contact provides counsel for the cluster and helps the peer mentor and students in the cluster explore academic issues related to cluster theme.

Clusters develop a project in UNIV 101 related to the LIFE cluster theme. The final project is a culminating group project that enables students to synthesize work they have been addressing in the UNIV 101 course as well as its connections to the other cluster courses.

Research Methods

Since the LIFE program began in 2000, it has been assessed using four methods: (a) student evaluations completed at the end of the fall semester, (b) a student needs survey at matriculation, (c) a comparison of students' demographic information and GPAs with non-LIFE students, and (d) faculty and peer mentor surveys completed at the end of fall semester. The student evaluations consist of a 70-item questionnaire with a portion focusing on UNIV 101 to evaluate satisfaction and perceived gains from the course.

Findings

Data collected over the past four years have shown that students are overwhelmingly positive about LIFE, citing the positive impact of LIFE and UNIV 101 on both their academic and social experience. In fall 2002, 85% of those responding to the survey said both programs enhanced their ability to collaborate with others, 75% said the program helped them make connections between their courses and the world, and 71% said they took initiative to get answers to questions.

As a program that seeks to provide academic and psychosocial transitions into the college environment, students perceived it to be a success. The majority of students said that the LIFE program helped them acquire skills that will prepare them for future courses, clarified the major they had or hoped to have, and helped them feel like they belonged in classes and the UD community. The vast majority of LIFE students were also very strong in their support of their living-learning community in the residence halls. They reported that living near other students in their cluster helped them form study groups, feel connected to peers, and feel like they belong at UD. Academic data tend to support the hypothesis that LIFE students perform better than non-LIFE peers (see Table 1).

Table 1
Academic Characteristics of First-Year Students, Fall 2000-2002

	Fall 2000 Cohort		Fall 2001 Cohort		Fall 2002 Cohort	
	LIFE ($n = 119$)	Non-LIFE ($n = 2583$)	LIFE ($n = 200$)	Non-LIFE ($n = 2712$)	LIFE ($n = 207$)	Non-LIFE ($n = 2848$)
Mean SAT	1151	1126**	1142	1134	1149	1143
Predicted grade index	2.82	2.74**	2.76	2.74	2.79	2.80
Fall 2000 GPA end of term	2.87	2.76				
Spring 2001 GPA end of term	2.91	2.73**				
Fall 2001 GPA end of term			2.78	2.73		
Spring 2002 GPA end of term	2.91	2.86	2.79	2.76		
Fall 2002 GPA end of term					2.92	2.78**
Spring 2003 GPA end of term, cumulative	2.97	2.91	2.89	2.88	2.93	2.80**

Note. Predicted Grade Average based on high school grades and SAT scores. Analyses above omit students with GPA = 0.0.
** $p < .01$

The majority of LIFE students say they would recommend the LIFE program to others. When asked what UNIV 101 activities built upon their learning, many respondents mention the final cluster project, guest speakers, and field trips. LIFE students say they benefited from the living-learning environment in which they studied and socialized with peers. The tight-knit living-learning communities allow students a level of comfort in which they could meet professors, ask each other questions, and raise their level of academic self-concept that helps guide them in their first-year success.

Peer mentor evaluations also point to successful UNIV 101 experiences. For example, peer mentors indicate that they gained a sense of leadership and learned how to be more organized and well prepared. One peer mentor says that she enjoyed developing skills in her students that will make them more successful in whatever they do.

The overwhelming majority of respondents say they feel prepared and receive adequate resources to teach the UNIV 101 course. Peer mentors believe that first-year students gain important knowledge about the campus and opportunities to develop peer friendships.

Contact

Meghan Biery
LIFE Program Coordinator
212 Gore Hall
University of Delaware
Newark, DE 19716
Phone: (302) 831-3330
Fax: (302) 831-2029
E-mail: mbiery@udel.edu

Additional Contributor:
Martha Carothers
Associate Director
Office of Undergraduate Studies

# University of Massachusetts Boston

The Institution

The University of Massachusetts Boston (UMB) is a public, urban university in the city of Boston serving approximately 10,000 undergraduates and 3,000 graduate students. It grants four-year undergraduate degrees as well as master's and doctoral degrees. All students commute. Full-time, first-year students entering with no transfer credits constitute approximately one third of entering students in a typical fall semester. The undergraduate student body includes 58% women and 40% people of color (approximately 18% African American, 14% Asian, 8% Hispanic/Latino, and 1% Native American). The average age is about 26.

The Seminar

Since the fall of 2000, students entering UMB with fewer than 30 credits have been required to take a first-year seminar (FYS). First-year seminars are four-credit academic seminars on a wide variety of topics that integrate seven capabilities into a content-driven course. The capabilities include careful reading, critical thinking, clear writing, oral presentation, teamwork, information technology and academic self-assessment. Each FYS is capped at 25 students and ordinarily has an advisor and a student mentor attached to it. Offered by many departments, they represent a wide range of content areas with titles such as: *Religion, Politics, Sex and Violence; Self and Other in Modern French Literature; Women Between Cultures; Technology and the Soul; Athenian Democracy; Marvelous Fictions: Latin American Novel; Black Consciousness;* and *Privacy.* A few of the seminars count toward majors, but most do not. Part-time faculty teach approximately half of the 52 sections offered each year.

The primary course goals include helping students practice the seven required capabilities as listed above, get to know UMB, and gain competence in the subject matter. Related to reading, writing, and critical thinking, students are expected to produce at least one five-page analytical paper that would be acceptable for UMB's Writing Proficiency Requirement portfolio.

Institution Profile:

Boston, MA

Public, Four-Year

11,124

Academic w/Variable
    Content

Learning Community

Since fall 2003, students entering with no previous college credits, regardless of their ages, have been required to take an FYS paired with English 101. Pairs are created primarily based on schedule compatibility (i.e., contiguous courses) and faculty willingness to teach a paired section. (Some faculty prefer a more seasoned group of students because students in paired courses tend to be younger.) Students in paired courses thus spend seven hours per week together, move from one classroom to another as a group, and sometimes have teachers who are working with shared course content. About 23 pairs, which accounts for nearly 40% of all FYS sections, are offered each year, mostly in the fall. The primary goal of the pairings is to help students gain a sense of community and feel more connected to UMB, especially since all students commute. We encourage faculty to collaborate on course content and pedagogical strategies and reward their efforts with a modest stipend to compensate for the added time required. About one fourth of the faculty each semester are willing and able to do this.

Research Design

At the end of the fall 2003 semester, the Seminars Assessment Committee (SAC) conducted a survey of students in the paired courses. It was completed by students in 17 of the 20 paired sections ($N = 298$). Among the questions addressed were whether and how students spent time with each other outside the classroom, whether they made new friends, whether they found the pairing academically beneficial, and whether they thought we should require paired courses for new first-year students in the future.

Among the 20 paired sections were five faculty teams that collaborated in developing their course materials and classroom activities. Student experiences in collaborating and non-collaborating pairs are compared here. SAC also held debriefing sessions both during and at the end of the semester for all paired faculty during which both collaborating and non-collaborating faculty discussed their experiences.

Findings

Our research indicates that faculty collaboration has a greater impact on student success than the mere pairing of classes. Most students in paired courses appear to have had a positive social experience. Eighty-three percent spent time with a classmate outside the classroom, either on or off campus or both. Eighty-eight percent reported making friends in the class. Faculty collaboration seemed to have no effect on whether students spent time together outside of class: 82.8% of those in classes in which faculty collaborated reported spending time with classmates outside of class compared to 82.9% of students in classes in which the faculty did not collaborate. Faculty collaboration did, however, correlate with a significantly higher probability that students would report making friends in the class: 93.9% compared to 84.9% ($\chi^2 = 5.058$, $df = 1$, $p < .03$).

A total of 59% of the students reported that they benefited academically from the pairing. This effect was significantly more pronounced in the courses in which faculty collaborated. Within these collaborated courses, 70.7% of students reported academic benefit compared to 52.8% of students in courses without faculty collaboration ($\chi^2 = 8.781$, $df = 1$, $p < .01$). Two types of academic benefits emerged: (a) feeling comfortable in the learning context, which translated into being able to ask classmates for help or speak up, and (b) being supported in learning the course content.

Finally, we wondered whether students thought that paired classes should be required for new students. Two thirds of respondents checked either "yes'" or "probably" to the question about whether pairings should be required. Another 14% said they were not sure. Twenty percent were against pairing, checking either "probably not" or "no." Students in courses in which the faculty had collaborated were significantly more likely to support required pairings for new first-year students: 77.8% compared to 60.1% of those in courses without collaboration ($\chi^2 = 9.818$, $df = 2$, $p < .01$, comparing "yes" or "probably yes," "not sure," and "no" or "probably not").

Conclusion

In all, merely having students attend the same classes together was not as effective as having students attend faculty-collaborated courses. Based on these responses, we have decided to continue requiring paired courses for zero-credit entering students at UMB, and we are encouraging faculty to collaborate.

Contact

Estelle Disch
Professor of Sociology, First Year Seminar Coordinator
Chair, Seminars Assessment Committee
Department of Sociology
University of Massachusetts Boston
100 Morrissey Boulevard
Boston, MA 02125-3393
Phone: (617) 287-6256
Fax: (617) 287-6288
E-mail: estelle.disch@umb.edu

 # University of North Carolina at Charlotte

The Institution

The University of North Carolina (UNC) at Charlotte is a four-year, public institution located in the urban region of Charlotte, NC. The University is one of the 16 constituent institutions that comprise The University of North Carolina. Founded in 1946, UNC Charlotte is one of the fastest growing universities in the state. The University is classified as a Doctoral/Research – Intensive institution, enrolling 19,605 students (15,694 undergraduates and 3,911 graduate students). The first-year class accounts for 2,500 students, and the majority of students are full-time. The undergraduate student body is increasingly traditional, with an average age of 18 years for first-year students. The University serves a diverse student population. The race/ethnicity of the students is as follows: White, non-Hispanic (74%); African American, non-Hispanic (15%); Asian/Pacific Islanders (5%); Hispanic (2%), American Indian/Alaskan Native (0.3%); non-resident alien (3%). Approximately 71% of the entering first-year class live on campus their first semester.

The Seminar

The first-year seminar course is a three-credit, graded, elective course offered through the College of Arts & Sciences (ARSC 1000). The course has been offered for more than 10 years, with approximately 30 sections being offered each fall. Each section is limited to 25 students. A diverse group of instructors, including student affairs professionals and faculty from a wide range of disciplines, teaches the course. Some sections are dedicated to specific student populations (e.g., athletes, participants in learning communities, and discipline-specific areas), but most sections are open to any new student. ARSC 1000 counts as a general elective course. The University has recently begun offering some sections in the spring semester.

This extended orientation course is intended to provide students with information and tools that will help them gain a better

---

Institution Profile:

Charlotte, NC

Public, Four-Year

19,605

Extended Orientation

Learning Community

awareness of campus resources and services, encourage them to get connected to the university community, and enhance strategies for successful academic and personal growth. The course asks students to identify personal strengths and weaknesses and emphasizes team building among students. While there is variation among the individual instructors, most instructors stress the following goals:

- Introduce students to UNC Charlotte and provide ongoing support and orientation during the transition from high school to college
- Build supportive relationships in the classroom and help students connect with peers and instructors
- Encourage discussion and active participation
- Incorporate a variety of skills essential to academic and personal success (i.e., written communication, oral communication, self-reflection, organization, critical thinking, and the ability to synthesize ideas and information)
- Empower students with the skills and knowledge necessary for a successful college experience
- Encourage students to take greater responsibility for their own behavior and learning
- Assist students in identifying and participating in the co-curricular life of the University

Specific course requirements vary by individual instructor, but most require attendance and class participation, journals, reflection papers, group projects, and often a service-learning project.

Research Design

UNC Charlotte uses a longitudinal, multiple source data collection model as an integral part of its research design. Since 1997, on a yearly basis, all new first-year students are identified and entered into a dataset as a cohort group. Data from other University systems pertaining to the cohort are subsequently imported into the dataset. The database documents student demographic profiles and other pre-enrollment data from the student information system, results from a statewide entering first-year student survey (similar to CIRP Freshman Survey), and participation in structured first-year programs. At the end of each semester, academic performance information is added to the dataset and then analyzed across the pooled data for outcomes. The system is flexible enough to incorporate data from periodically administered surveys such as National Survey of Student Engagement (NSSE) and other locally developed instruments.

Findings

Since instituting this approach in 1997, we have demonstrated significant gains in a number of outcome areas associated with the first-year seminar. One outcome is higher semester grade point averages (GPAs) among both commuting and residential students who take the seminar ($p < .05$). At the end of the first semester, commuting first-year students who took the seminar earned a 2.79 GPA compared to a 2.42 GPA for non-seminar students. Among residential students, the differences in first semester GPA were also significant. Seminar students earned a first-semester GPA of 2.75 compared to a 2.38 GPA for non-seminar students.

Another statistically significant outcome of first-year seminar participation is increased graduation and retention rates ($p < .05$). Commuting students who participate in the seminar graduate from the institution within four years at a rate of 28% compared to 17% for non-seminar students. Among first-year students residing on campus, 84% of those taking the seminar return for their second year, whereas only 79% of those who do not take the seminar return. We have found these outcomes to be consistent over time.

One of the benefits of our research model is the ability to incorporate data from other sources like locally developed instruments or NSSE. Locally developed environmental assessments address outcomes associated with student-student, student-faculty, and student-staff relationships; involvement in other structured university programs such as orientation; and external environmental factors (i.e., the number of hours worked per week and place of residence). We currently maintain a three-year cycle for participating either in the NSSE or locally developed instruments to assess several of these more complex outcomes.

Using this methodology, we have found significant positive outcomes associated with first-year seminar participation. Commuting first-year seminar students are more likely to experience positive relationships with faculty, spend more time preparing for class, participate in co-curricular activities, and feel like the University is supporting them socially. First-year seminar students living on campus reported that they are more likely to come to class having completed assignments or readings, feel that the University provides them with both academic and social support, and discuss career plans with faculty (Table 1).

Outcomes of these varied assessments are shared regularly within the first-year seminar teaching community and wider audiences including other faculty, senior administration, parents, prospective students, and our board of trustees. Based largely on these generated outcomes, we have successfully articulated the need for additional resources to double the size of our program and have been able to modify our faculty training programs to further enhance our first-year seminars.

Table 1

Outcomes Associated with First-Year Seminar Participation for Fall 2000 Cohort

	Commuters	
	Participants	Non-Participants
More likely to discuss ideas with faculty outside of class	64%	52%
More likely to spend more than 10 hours per week preparing for class	50%	43%
More likely to participate weekly in co-curricular activities	45%	25%
More likely to feel that the University provides them with support to thrive socially	27%	16%
	Residents	
	Participants	Non-Participants
More likely to go to class having completed reading or assignments	92%	70%
More likely to feel that the University provides them academic support	72%	69%
More likely to discuss career plans with a faculty member	92%	77%

Note. Data gathered from NSSE 2001.
$^*p < .05$

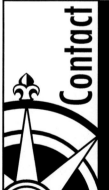

Anita N. Blowers
Director, Office of Student Success and Retention
University of North Carolina at Charlotte
9201 University City Boulevard
Charlotte, NC 28223-0001
Phone: (704) 687-6074
Fax: (704) 687-2616
E-mail: anblower@uncc.edu

Additional Contributor:

Theodore W. Elling
Associate Vice Chancellor for Student Affairs

178

University of Texas at El Paso

The Institution

The University of Texas at El Paso (UTEP) is a doctoral, research-intensive, four-year public institution located on the US-Mexico border. UTEP's total fall 2003 enrollment was 18,542 students; more than 2,300 of them were first-time, first-year students. The majority of the student population is Hispanic (71%). More than 10% of the student population are international students; 9.8% are Mexican, and 2.4% come from some other country. Additional student populations include 12.8% White, 2.4% African American, 1.2% Asian American, and 0.3% Native American. The great majority of UTEP's bi-national student population is nontraditional; the average undergraduate age is 24. Ninety-eight percent commute, and more than 80% work. In addition, many have family responsibilities or are the first in their families to attend college (54%).

The Seminar

UTEP has offered its first-year seminar, UNIV 1301 *Seminar in Critical Inquiry*, since 1999. The seminar is a three-credit academic course with variable content related to each instructor's area of expertise. Students may select from such diverse themes as "Voices of Change: Social Protest in the Sixties," "Fictional Women Detectives," "Nuclear Enviroethics," and "Business Environment in the Borderplex." College transition and success skills are addressed through the theme. The seminar is one of two courses that fulfill the institutionally designated option of the University's core curriculum. Currently, 70% of all full-time, first-year students enroll in the seminar in their first semester. Sections are capped at 25 students.

Many seminar courses are offered in learning communities for the general population and for special populations such as the Circles of Learning for Entering Students (CircLES) program for pre-science and pre-engineering majors. Seminars in ·learning communities are linked to one, two, or three other courses and

Institution Profile:

El Paso, TX

Public, Four-Year

18,542

Academic w/Variable
    Content

Learning Community

often act as the linking course. For example, the seminar themed "Law for Beginners" is teamed with "History of the US Since 1865." The seminar instructor selects case law that connects with key events discussed in the history course.

An instructional team consisting of an instructor, librarian, and peer leader (i.e., upper-division student) teaches each seminar. Instructors may be full-time faculty or staff, with a master's or terminal degree. Though the theme for each section varies, all must address the same five goals:

1. Strengthen students' academic performance and facilitate their transition to college
2. Enhance students' essential academic skills
3. Increase student-student and student-faculty interaction both in and outside the classroom
4. Encourage students' self-assessment and goal clarification
5. Increase students' involvement with UTEP activities and resources

To teach the seminar, instructors must submit a proposal identifying the theme and describing how the section will address course goals. Proposals are accepted based on academic merit.

Research Design

The seminar assessment strategy focuses on the development and longitudinal tracking of student cohorts, using data from UTEP's Student Information System. Through student self-evaluations, anonymous surveys, and focus groups, qualitative analyses are produced to complement the quantitative results. Peer leaders and instructors complete surveys that report on student progress and suggest topics for future workshops. In total, this evaluation effort addresses all seminar goals. The strategy is based on the success and collaboration of the evaluation efforts of the National Science Foundation-supported Model Institutions for Excellence grant, the CircLES program, and the University College. Until recently, assessment of the seminar for CircLES students had been tracked separately. Assessment of all seminar sections is now part of a larger University College assessment. Collectively, these efforts address the impact made on student retention, success (measured by GPA), skills, and graduation.

Findings

Entering student cohorts examined over the past five years show that students who enroll in the seminar demonstrate higher retention rates and GPAs than their counterparts who do not complete the seminar. Three indicators of seminar success were selected as baseline measures in the longitudinal study of program effectiveness: (a) first-time seminar enrollment, (b) retention rates, and (c) cumulative GPA.

Since the seminar's inception, the number of students enrolled has more than doubled, from 1,265 in the 1999-2000 academic year to 2,957 in the 2002-2003 academic year. The percentage of first-time, full-time first-year students enrolled in the course increased from 44% in 1999-2000 to 70% in 2003-2004. During this same period, the retention rate of those enrolled in the seminar remained relatively steady, between 72% and 74%. The one-year retention rates for those who never enrolled in the seminar were considerably lower, between 43% and 61% (See Table 1).

Table 1
One-Year Student Retention by Cohort (Fall 1999-2002)

	Entered fall/Enrolled in seminar in fall	Entered fall/ Never enrolled in seminar
Fall 1999	74.1%	60.9%
Fall 2000	74.3%	45.6%
Fall 2001	73.4%	42.7%
Fall 2002	72.0%	52.5%

$p < 0.01$

Though the course is recommended for all first-year students, certain groups of students are required or strongly encouraged to enroll in the seminar during their first semester at UTEP. These groups are provisionally admitted students, lower proficiency English as a Second Language (ESL) students, and pre-science/pre-engineering students. An analysis of covariance, to control for the external factors of SAT score, ethnicity, and gender, confirm the findings that GPA is positively affected for those taking the seminar during their first semester (Table 2).

Table 2
First-Term Average GPA Based on Analysis of Covariance

	Entered fall /Enrolled in seminar in fall	Entered fall / Never enrolled in seminar
Fall 1999	2.72	2.16
Fall 2000	2.76	1.85
Fall 2001	2.78	1.99
Fall 2002	2.72	2.33
Fall 2003	2.76	2.18

Note. Does not include students without an SAT score. Effects of ethnicity and gender have been removed.
$p < 0.01$

Data from surveys administered from 2000 through 2002 indicate that most students reported that their academic survival skills, sense of comfort, campus participation, and use of essential student services improved as a result of the seminar (Table 3).

Table 3
Student-Reported Seminar Outcomes for First-Time, Full-Time, First-Year Students (2000-2002)

	Fall 2000 ($n = 382$)	Fall 2001 ($n = 607$)	Fall 2002 ($n = 892$)
Percentage of seminar completers who report. . .			
Their academic survival skills increased	83.1%	80.8%	75.1%
They feel more comfortable at UTEP	71.4%	75.5%	73.9%
The seminar helps first-year students learn to succeed at UTEP	74.0%	76.7%	75.8%
Having participated in at least three campus activities	74.6%	61.2%	61.3%
Using at least two essential support services	90.8%	95.4%	92.7%

Contact

Dorothy Ward
Director, Entering Student Program
Burges Hall, Room 201
500 West University
University of Texas at El Paso
El Paso, TX 79968
Phone: (915) 747-8439
Fax: (915) 747-6496
E-mail: dpward@utep.edu

Additional Contributors:

Maggy Smith
Dean, University College

Cathy Willermet
Assistant Director, University Studies

Ann Darnell
Assistant Director, MIE Program

Diana Guerrero
Director, Institutional Evaluation, Research, and Planning

Wheaton College

The Institution

Wheaton College is a highly selective, private, residential, four-year liberal arts undergraduate college of about 1,500 students. Wheaton is located in Norton, Massachusetts, between Boston and Providence, Rhode Island. In the fall 2003, students came from 45 states and 29 countries, and at least 98% were between 18 and 22 years of age. The gender distribution was about 64% women and 36% men, and about 12% of the students self-identified as ethnic minorities: Hispanic (3.9%), Asian (3%), African American (2.9%), Multiracial (1.8%), American Indian (0.4%), and Pacific Islander (0.1%). Wheaton admitted about 43% of its applicants, and approximately 45% of those students were in the top 10% of their high school class.

Institution Profile:

Norton, MA

Private, Four-Year

1,565

Academic w/Variable Content

The Seminar

Our first-year seminar program (FYS), entitled *Great Controversies,* is required for first-year students. The FYS has existed for more than 15 years and was re-approved in a review of the general educational requirements in December 2001. Each seminar is a one-credit academic course with variable content. The number of seminars offered depends on the size of the entering class, calculated so that there are no more than 18 students in any section.

Faculty instructors are drawn from every division and most departments of the college. Each section is built around a topic that reflects the instructor's choice of a controversial theme or issue related to his/her area of expertise. For instance, one seminar offered by an economist is entitled "Poverty in a Global Context"; another offered by a biologist is entitled, "Evolution, Genes, and Society." In these seminars, students certainly learn about the specific discipline; but they also hone important skills needed to succeed in college. These skills include careful reading, critical thinking, active participation in discussions, formal oral presentations, formal writing skills, library skills, and familiarity with information technologies. Central to the intellectual challenge of FYS is the idea that the topic of each section may be approached and understood from multiple perspectives and that these different ways of understanding often lead to controversy.

However, the seminar experience begins before students arrive on campus. To prepare them for the intellectual challenge they will find at college, all students complete the same summer reading and writing assignment. Then, as part of Orientation, students meet with their seminar section to talk about the summer reading, and attend a panel discussion in which faculty members, who have written essays on the reading, answer questions students develop within their small group meetings.

In almost all cases, the instructor also serves as the academic advisor to the students in her/his seminar. Attached to each seminar are two student preceptors, upperclass students who have been trained (through a half-credit course) to help students with course selection and issues such as time management. They are also available in the residence halls to direct students to campus resources they might need. The work of these preceptors frees up faculty advisors to address "higher level" concerns with students such as identifying goals and strategies for achieving them through college in general and Wheaton in particular. Each FYS is also assigned an administrative mentor, a staff person who serves as another advisor to students for general college issues. She or he is another point of contact with the institution, someone who is knowledgeable about the college and can be a resource for students.

Research Design

Evaluation of each FYS occurs in two venues. First, each FYS is evaluated by the students in that section. The evaluation instrument is the same for every section and is reviewed each year by the FYS steering committee (composed of faculty members currently teaching a FYS). The evaluation form asks questions about student learning for all the goals mentioned above. It also asks for information on the time students spend working on their FYS and how this compares to other courses they are taking. Information from these evaluations allows quantitative comparisons to be made between seminars. The evaluations also ask for comments from students that provide qualitative information on their experiences. Secondly, each faculty instructor is asked to evaluate, in narrative form, her/his FYS experience. Often, these evaluations and the information collected from the students are used in a May workshop for instructors who are preparing to teach a section of FYS the following fall.

Findings

This report focuses on selected responses from student evaluations rather than the narrative remarks submitted by the instructors. Below are some of the more interesting findings, followed by a few interpretive comments on the results. Each statement is followed by the percentage of respondents who agreed or agreed strongly with that item in fall 2003.

Several statements focused on the role of class discussions.

- "Class discussions in my seminar have been thought provoking." (88%)
- "The instructor encourages student discussion." (95%)
- "I participate in discussions in this course more than in other courses." (62%)
- "My participation has increased my confidence as a speaker." (55%)

These responses imply that faculty recognize the importance of encouraging discussion and preparing courses that make students engage in and think about the material. Nevertheless, it is also evident that we need to work with students throughout their academic careers to help them become more comfortable participating in formal discussions.

One particular item attempted to measure the success of the great controversies theme.

- "My FYS has helped me improve my ability to understand other people's positions." (78%)

Over the past few years, our focus on controversy has carefully tried to avoid the binary, win-lose, right-wrong aspect of controversy and, instead, replace it with the notion that most complex issues need to be viewed from several perspectives to be fully understood. This builds on a conscious attempt to help our students develop an appreciation for diversity in all its intellectual aspects.

The following statement addresses our writing goals:

- "My FYS has helped me improve my skills as a writer." (66%)

Each seminar focuses on student writing, but most students (with the exception of those who place out through AP credits) also take an English composition course. Currently, we are talking about ways to coordinate the writing work that goes on in the FYS more closely with the English writing classes.

The development of reading skills was also addressed.

- "My FYS has helped me develop the reading skills needed to do the work in the course." (69%)

Library skills were assessed with this item:

- "My FYS has helped my library skills." (70%)

This statement gets considerable attention from the librarians who are assigned to work with each seminar instructor to develop meaningful library assignments. It is through this collaboration, and the graded assignment that students undertake, that students get a significant introduction to how to use our library.

To assess the overall effectiveness of the course, students were asked to rate their section on a five-point scale; 69% gave their FYS one of the top two possible marks. This score is consistent with those found in many introductory courses throughout the College.

These results indicate that at a general level the course has been successful. However, like any course, there is always room for improvement. To facilitate that improvement, we hold a daylong workshop every May in which new and veteran instructors talk about what worked well and what was less successful. We follow that up with a few lunch meetings during the semester that provide an opportunity for faculty to talk about their seminars.

Contact

Gordon Weil
Associate Provost
Wheaton College
26 East Main St.
Norton, MA 02766
Phone: (508) 286-8230
Fax: (508) 286-8270
E-mail: Gweil@WheatonMa.edu

Index of Institutions by Category

Index of School Type and Affiliation

Two-Year Schools
Public

Four-Year Schools
Private

Public

Index of Seminar Types

Extended Orientation

Academic with Variable Content

Academic with Uniform Content

Basic Study Skills

Hybrid

Index of Learning Communities

Some or all of the seminar sections are linked to other courses.

Index of Outcomes

Academic Achievement / Grade Point Averages

Career/Life Planning

Effects on Faculty

Graduation Rates

Instructional/Grading Strategies

Library Use

Peer Relationships

Retention/Persistence

Social Justice and Gender Attitudes

Student Adjustment/Involvement

Student Satisfaction (with course or institution / meeting course objectives)

Student Self-Assessment

Index of Other Issues Considered

About the Editors

Barbara F. Tobolowsky is associate director of the National Resource Center for The First-Year Experience and Students in Transition. In this position, she has overall responsibility for the Center's research and publication efforts. Tobolowsky also teaches University 101 and several graduate seminars in the Higher Education Student Affairs program (HESA) at the University of South Carolina. She earned her doctorate from the University of California, Los Angeles in higher education and organizational change.

Bradley E. Cox is the coordinator of research and public information at the National Resource Center for The First-Year Experience and Students in Transition. He earned his bachelor's degree from the University of North Carolina at Chapel Hill and completed his master's in higher education administration and student affairs at the University of South Carolina in Columbia. Currently, he is the editor of the FYA-List, an electronic magazine/listserv dedicated to assessment of the first college year. His personal research interests include residential colleges and faculty-student interaction outside of the classroom.

Mary T. Wagner is a graduate assistant in research and publications. Prior to joining the National Resource Center, she spent nine years in various admissions and enrollment management settings at both public and private colleges in the South. Her most recent responsibilities as director of enrollment management and institutional research at Louisiana College included the design, implementation, and assessment of both advising programs for at-risk students and campus-wide retention initiatives. Wagner earned her bachelor's degree at the University of South Carolina and her master's degree in college student personnel at Bowling Green State University. Presently, she is a doctoral student in the higher education administration program at the University of South Carolina.

 **Other Titles From the National Resource Center**

Monograph No. 41. The 2003 National Survey on First-Year Seminars: Continuing Innovations in the Collegiate Curriculum. *Barbara F. Tobolowsky with Marla Mamrick and Bradley E. Cox.* This volume reports on the sixth triennial National Survey on First-Year Seminars. Data from more than 600 colleges and universities are analyzed to offer information on the structure, content, and administration of these courses. Changes to the survey capture new information on innovative course practices including incorporating service-learning, linking the seminar with other courses, and teaching all or part of the seminar online. (2005). 128 pages. ISBN 1-889271-49-7. $35.00

Monograph No. 37. Proving and Improving, Volume II: Tools and Techniques for Assessing the First College Year. *Randy L. Swing, Editor. Produced in association with the Policy Center on the First Year of College.* This second volume of *Proving and Improving* offers overviews of commercially available instruments and provides case studies of qualitative assessment strategies. The monograph also includes a comprehensive introduction by Randy Swing, describing strategies for implementing an effective assessment effort, and a typology of assessment instruments that allows readers to identify and compare instruments geared to the issues and programs they want to assess. (2004). 230 pages. ISBN 1-889271-44-6. $35.00

Monograph No. 33. Proving and Improving: Strategies for Assessing the First College Year. *Randy L. Swing, Editor. Produced in association with the Policy Center on the First Year of College.* Outlines the essentials of effective assessment efforts, describes methods and strategies for assessment, and provides examples designed for institutions and specific programs. (2001). 144 pages. ISBN 1-889271-37-3. $20.00

Monograph No. 25. Exploring the Evidence, Volume II: Reporting Outcomes of First-Year Seminars. *Betsy O. Barefoot, Carrie Warnock, Michael Dickinson, Sharon Richardson, and Melissa Roberts, Editors. Produced with the financial support of the Houghton Mifflin Company.* Reviews research outcomes of 50 first-year seminars including improved retention and graduation rates, higher grade point averages, increased levels of student satisfaction, and improved teaching strategies. (1998). 120 pages. ISBN 1-889271-25-X $30.00

Journal of The First-Year Experience and Students in Transition. A semiannual, refereed journal providing current research and scholarship on the first college year and other student transitions. The Journal publishes definitive scholarship by respected higher education researchers about the factors that relate to student success and survival. ISSN 1053-203X. Subscription $40.00 (2 issues). Back issues available upon request. Specify volume & number. $20.00

Primer for Research on the College Student Experience. *Dorothy S. Fidler and Jean M. Henscheid.* Offers an overview of strategies for designing, conducting, and publishing research on the college student experience. (2002). 68 pages. $15.00

Use the order form on the next page to order any of these titles from the National Resource Center.

Use this form to order additional copies of this monograph or to order other titles from the National Resource Center for The First-Year Experience & Students in Transition.

Prices advertised in this publication are subject to change.

Item	Quantity	Price	Total
Monograph 42. *Exploring the Evidence, Vol. III*		$35.00	
Monograph 41. *The 2003 National Survey on First-Year Seminars*		$35.00	
Monograph 37. *Proving & Improving, Vol. II*		$35.00	
Monograph 33. *Proving & Improving*		$20.00	
Monograph 25. *Exploring the Evidence, Vol. II*		$30.00	
Journal of The First-Year Experience and Students in Transition		$40.00	
Primer for Research on the College Student Experience		$15.00	

Shipping Charges:	**Order Amount**	**Shipping Cost**	Shipping & Handling	
U.S.	$1 - $50	$ 6.50 US		
	$51 - $150	$10.00 US		
	over $150	$15.00 US		
Foreign	For orders shipped outside of the United States, customers will be billed exact shipping charges plus a $5.00 processing fee. Fax or e-mail us to obtain a shipping estimate. Be sure to include a list of items you plan to purchase and to specify your preference for Air Mail or UPS Delivery.		Total	

Name _____   Department _____

Institution _____   Telephone _____

Address _____

City _____   State/Province _____   Postal Code _____

E-mail Address _____

❑ Please send me e-mail announcements about upcoming NRC events and available resources in the future.

Select your option payable to the University of South Carolina Federal ID 57-6001153:

❑ Check Enclosed   ❑ Institutional Purchase Order   Purchase Order No._____

Credit Card: ❑ VISA   ❑ MasterCard   ❑ DISCOVER

Card No. _____   Expiration Date _____

Name of Cardholder _____

Billing Address _____

City _____   State/Province _____   Postal Code _____

Signature _____

Mail this form to: National Resource Center for The First-Year Experience & Students in Transition, University of South Carolina, 1728 College Street, Columbia, SC 29208. Phone (803) 777-6229. Fax (803) 777-4699. E-mail: burtonp@sc.edu